THE CLEOPATRA
TEACHER RULES

Also by the Author

Classroom Management: A Guide for Urban School Teachers

The 12 Laws of Urban School Leadership: A Principal's Guide for Initiating Effective Change

The Hard Truth: Problems and Issues in Urban School Reform

The Warrior Principal: New Leadership for Urban Schools

THE CLEOPATRA TEACHER RULES

Effective Strategies for Engaging Students and Increasing Achievement

Sean B. Yisrael

ROWMAN & LITTLEFIELD
Lanham • Boulder • New York • Toronto • Plymouth, UK

Published by Rowman & Littlefield
4501 Forbes Boulevard, Suite 200, Lanham, Maryland 20706
www.rowman.com

10 Thornbury Road, Plymouth PL6 7PP, United Kingdom

British Library Cataloguing in Publication Information Available

Library of Congress Cataloging-in-Publication Data

Yisrael, Sean B.
The Cleopatra teacher rules : effective strategies for engaging students and increasing achievement / Sean B. Yisrael.
pages cm
Includes bibliographical references.
ISBN 978-1-4758-0860-5 (cloth : alk. paper)—ISBN 978-1-4758-0861-2 (pbk. : alk. paper)—ISBN 978-1-4758-0862-9 (electronic) 1. Teaching—United States. 2. Public schools—United States. I. Title.
LB1025.3.Y57 2014
371.102—dc23
2013044410

∞™ The paper used in this publication meets the minimum requirements of American National Standard for Information Sciences Permanence of Paper for Printed Library Materials, ANSI/NISO Z39.48-1992.

Printed in the United States of America

CONTENTS

ACKNOWLEDGMENTS

First and foremost, I'd like to give all praise and honor to YHWH: He is the creator of the heavens, earth, sea, and all that there is. All glory belongs unto him only.

Special thanks go out to three dynamic educators: Marla Mitchell, Deyon Johnson, and Angela Harriston. I thank you for assisting me during the peer review process of this book. Your collective feedback and critique helped to make this book better. I am truly grateful.

To all the public schoolteachers and advocates who work tirelessly to serve students and parents—this one is for you. Please continue to stand strong for public education, and never give up on our youth, regardless of their personal, family, or community circumstances. I hope this book will serve as a tool that will help improve the educational practices and experiences for both teachers and students.

INTRODUCTION

The idea to write this book came to me in the fall of 2012 while researching another book I was writing titled *The Warrior Principal: New Leadership for Urban Schools.* That particular book combined school leadership principles with effective strategies of war as a guide for principals to use while spearheading the school reform process in an urban school model. To write that book, I studied several military figures and war strategists from the past and present. During that process one unlikely person stood out to me and truly sparked my interest.

This particular person from antiquity intrigued me for several reasons. First, the person was a woman. During her life, there were very few prominent female leaders, and fewer with any significant power and respect among her contemporaries. Second, this particular woman was ruler of one of ancient history's most powerful and well-known kingdoms. This nation's fame, wealth, and past accomplishments are still being studied today. Last, her life has become the stuff of legends; the mere mentioning of her name sparks controversy, intrigue, and mystery to this day. The person I'm referring to is none other than Cleopatra VII, the ancient queen of Egypt.

There has been a lot said and written about Cleopatra over the years. Some have characterized her as being self-serving, conniving, immoral, and unscrupulous, but she is best known historically for being a seductress: Her romances with Julius Caesar and Mark Antony are legendary, and will be forever linked to her legacy and theirs. Cleopatra's life and death have inspired numerous books, movies, and folklore. Detailed accounts of her life are still debated by historians to this day. After intense study of Cleopatra, I've learned that there is a deeper level of understanding regarding her story that can be useful for today's teaching professionals. Cleopatra may be viewed differently by different people, but despite her imperfections—and the controversy, myths, and speculations surrounding the events of her life and death—many of the principles she used to independently rule Egypt can also be transposed and used by public schoolteachers to manage and organize their classrooms effectively, and to increase student achievement.

I hold to the premise that true education doesn't happen in a vacuum. Authentic teaching and learning not only take place in school buildings and in classrooms, but also during everyday life experiences and events. During my study of Cleopatra, I uncovered several parallels that exist between her life experiences and those of today's public schoolteachers. More importantly, I also discovered certain principles, or rules, that Cleopatra utilized during her reign that kept her in power. If adopted and used appropriately, these rules can also make public schoolteachers more effective at performing their primary job function—educating students.

Most of what is known about Cleopatra comes from her detractors who lived within or supported the ancient Roman Empire. Their accounts paint a cruel picture of Cleopatra, but despite all that was written, there is no denying that she was a master in the art of engaging people. Whether it was one person or a group of people, Cleopatra was effectively able to draw people to her. In fact, her life and legacy depended on her ability to effectively engage her target audience, whether it was Caesar, Antony, or the people of Egypt.

At the most basic level, being able to engage a person, or group of people, simply means that you have their complete attention; you have their attention because they have a strong interest in you, or they desire to hear what you have to say. If you are able to capture people's attention, then you are more likely to influence their behavior or thinking in some way.

Cleopatra was not only good at captivating people's attention, she was effective at using her influence to move individuals in one direction or another—usually in the direction that mostly benefited her interests. The ancient historian Plutarch once wrote the following about Cleopatra:

> The contact of her presence, if you lived with her, was irresistible; the attraction of her person, joining with the charm of her conversation and the character that attended all she said and did, was something bewitching. It was pleasure to merely hear the sound of her voice.

Just like with Cleopatra, public schoolteachers need a firm understanding in the art of engaging people. This is critical for their survival in the profession. Among all the people whom public schoolteachers interact with throughout the course of a school year, the students they see each day in their classrooms are the ones for whom having the skills for effective engagement is most critical. The students are the sole reason why the teaching profession exists. Therefore, the fate of all teachers will forever be linked to students. This means the outcomes that students produce will always reflect on the work that teachers do, making student engagement that much more important. So despite Cleopatra's noted imperfections, this book focuses on her strategies for engagement that can also be beneficial for public schoolteachers.

In *The Schools Our Children Deserve,* Alfie Kohn warns us by saying, "The most immediate and pressing issue for students, and teachers, is not low achievement but student disengagement." Mr. Kohn understands that it is increasingly becoming difficult to capture students' attention in K–12 classrooms.

We're currently living in the age of information technology. It has permeated every aspect of our lives from the way we communicate to how we entertain ourselves. We are constantly bombarded with messages from various media sources competing for our attention. The average student has access to technology, information, and the most current news literally at his or her fingertips. Smartphones, iPads, social media, instant messaging, and other mechanisms are a normal part of their daily lives. If not channeled properly, the technology students have available to them today can serve as a distraction, and a stumbling block for teachers who aren't able to properly engage their students.

This problem is compounded for teachers who work in urban public school districts because they work with higher concentrations of students who come from families who live in poverty or in a low socioeconomic status. These students present more challenges to the learning process because many of them are deficient in one or more of their basic needs (i.e., food, clothing, shelter, or emotional support), often lack adequate parental support (i.e., single parent homes, unstable living arrangements, or limited extended family support), or they are adversely affected by negative influences that exist within the communities where they live (e.g., gangs, drugs, alcoholism, or extreme violence)—and sometimes a combination of all the three.

This doesn't mean that students from low socioeconomic status can't learn; it just means the challenges will be greater for the people who are responsible for educating them—making student engagement an even bigger factor for teachers working in such school districts. If teachers aren't able to effectively engage their students over a prolonged period (one calendar school year), then they will be unable to deliver a quality education. Students will become bored and disinterested, or they may give up and stop coming to school completely.

Student engagement is arguably the most critical factor for all teachers. It affects every aspect of their jobs from classroom management to standardized testing. It also affects students' morale, effort, participation, achievement, and their overall attitude about school and learning. A teacher's inability to engage his or her students could literally mean an early exit from the profession—and even worse, it ultimately means low-achieving students.

THE STRUCTURE OF THIS BOOK

While studying Cleopatra's life, I was able to identify several strategies that were critical for her governance of Egypt. When modified and adapted, Cleopatra's strategies can also be used by public schoolteachers to help improve how they engage students, deliver instruction, and increase their overall effectiveness as education professionals. I've coined these as the Cleopatra Teacher Rules. Queen Cleopatra used these rules on individuals such as Julius Caesar and Mark Antony, and on mass audiences like the people of Syria and Egypt. Each of the rules in this book have been adjusted so public schoolteachers can use them to enhance their students' classroom experiences.

Every chapter highlights one of Cleopatra's rules as they relate to the experience of most public schoolteachers today. Each chapter is then broken down into three sections: orientation, interpretation, and keys to teaching. In the first section, *orientation,* I chronicle specific

events and people in Queen Cleopatra's life. Although this section provides plenty of entertainment value, the true purpose of this section is
to expose the reader to the circumstances of Cleopatra's time, and how
she was able to adjust to them. This allows the reader to make connections and understand how and why the Cleopatra Rules were developed.

The second section, *interpretation,* describes the commonalities and
parallels that exist between Cleopatra and today's public schoolteachers. This section provides context for understanding how the rules apply
to the work a public schoolteacher performs on a daily basis. This section also helps the reader understand the student engagement practices
and teaching principles discussed in the following section.

The final and arguably most important section of each chapter is
called *keys to teaching.* This section discusses the important student
engagement, teaching concepts, and strategies that public schoolteachers can incorporate in their own practices. I focus specifically on the
overall purpose and meaning behind the concept and the implications
that each teacher rule has on the teaching and learning process in K–12
classrooms. I also discuss specific strategies public schoolteachers can
use that will positively affect their overall performance, self-efficacy,
and overall classroom learning environment. This section is practical for
teachers, regardless of the content area, grade level, or school context
(i.e., urban, rural, private, or suburban school) they work in.

*The Cleopatra Teacher Rules: Effective Strategies for Engaging Stu-
dents and Increasing Achievement* is a provocative and unconventional
approach to improving teacher quality and effectiveness, and increasing
student achievement. This book is not about some new theory, pro-
gram, fad, or "innovation" in education. In a unique way, this book gets
at the root of what effective teachers do, and what quality education
should look like in public schools. This book puts emphasis on timeless
teaching principles that all teachers can use, serving as a resource for
teachers of varying degrees of experience and backgrounds. I do not
focus on specific subjects, curriculum, or programs that should be
taught, but rather on how teaching can best be done.

New teachers may use this book as a preparation tool to inform them
of what to expect upon accepting a new teaching position in a public
school district. It will also give them insight on how to better serve
students with various ability levels and backgrounds. Veteran teachers

can use this book as a personal development resource, helping them to sharpen their skills and improve their practice and overall instructional delivery. Whichever is the case, the tenets described in each chapter will arm all teachers with a comprehensive set of skills that will increase their individual chances of success and increase student achievement in the process. They will have knowledge of the most critical areas in which to focus, and the methods to use to obtain success for themselves and their students.

Some of the student engagement strategies and principles for effective teaching mentioned are best practices that are recognized and accepted by the education profession at large, while others may seem to be somewhat unconventional. The tenets of this book challenge conventional theories and move teachers toward different paradigms for engaging students. Most importantly, this book will help teachers define their practice, and take more ownership over the activities and events that occur in their classrooms.

Being able to engage and effectively teach students at all levels will make each individual teacher the queen (or king) of their kingdom (classroom). They will be able to create a rich learning environment where students' potential can blossom. This is the essence of effective teaching, and the basic premise for the Cleopatra Teacher Rules.

1

CRITICAL ISSUES AFFECTING PUBLIC SCHOOLTEACHERS

Many factors directly affect the work of all public schoolteachers. Some factors stem from state and federal mandates, while others come from local and community stakeholders. It doesn't matter where or how these factors are generated. The important thing to understand is that all of the factors directly affect the teaching and learning process and the work that teachers do each day. For public schoolteachers to have success and create positive outcomes for students, they need to be keenly aware of all the factors surrounding them. Awareness and understanding of the factors adversely affecting their profession will not only inform their decision making, it will also help them to navigate around pitfalls that derail many good teachers every year.

ORIENTATION[1]

When Alexander the Great died in 323 BC, his empire was split among several of his generals. One such general, a distant cousin named Ptolemy, assumed control of Egypt. Ptolemy was a Greek of Macedonian heritage, but upon becoming ruler of Egypt, he thought it wise to claim to be a successor of the ancient pharaohs, so he borrowed their symbols

---

1. The text in this section is a paraphrased narrative derived from facts presented by Roller (2010), Tyldesley (2008), Flamarion (1993), and Sapet (2007).

and rituals to win the support of the Egyptian people. This was used as a tool to establish his Ptolemaic dynasty.

By the time of Cleopatra's birth in 69 BC, Egypt was one of the wealthiest and most populous ports in the world. An estimated three million people lived there. Cleopatra's Greek ancestors ruled over an Egypt that was the center of most technological, cultural, and philosophical developments known to the world at that time.

Cleopatra experienced a privileged upbringing. She was educated in science, the performing arts, and mathematics; she had private teachers and access to the Alexandria Library, which was the largest in the world at that time. It was said to have contained over 600,000 scrolls of all kinds. As an adult, Cleopatra spoke six different languages fluently. She ate the best foods; wore the best clothes (silks, pearls, and fine linen); and lived in a luxurious apartment within the royal palace complete with staff, servants, and bodyguards to care for her every need.

Despite living a privileged lifestyle within the palace walls, the threat of danger was always present. At a young age Cleopatra learned that her family members had murdered, poisoned, and stabbed their own relatives to advance to the throne. Whereas in some kingdoms royal succession passed through the oldest son, in Egypt the pharaoh chose his successor. Her father, Ptolemy XII, would select from his children. Cleopatra always needed to be on guard, watching her siblings, who were just as ambitious as she. Losing the contest for power could likely mean losing one's life. It was a struggle in which she couldn't afford to trust anyone.

Life beyond the palace walls was just as dangerous. The Ptolemaic dynasty was much less powerful than it had been in previous generations. The rulers had become increasingly greedy, weak, and corrupt. They spent lavishly on palaces in their own honor, and they used money to finance their personal feuds. By the time of Cleopatra's father's reign, many of the dynasty's North African, Balkan, and Syrian territories had broken away.

Cleopatra's father, Ptolemy XII, abetted the decline through profligate spending. He was known as the "flute player" because he would frequently get drunk and play his flute in the street until he passed out. While the royal family lived in luxury, ordinary Egyptians suffered greatly. In years of scarce rain, when the Nile didn't flood, fields were left dry and people starved. Conversely, excessive flooding could spread disease and kill livestock. As a result, the streets seethed with violence and unrest. The people who lived in Egypt (both Greeks and Egyptians) plotted to remove Ptolemy XII.

To remain in power, Ptolemy XII knew he needed to align with a powerful ally. That ally was Rome. In an attempt to maintain his throne, he made a deal with the Roman government. This began a long, complicated relationship in which Egypt would unsuccessfully struggle to maintain its independence. In 59 BC, when Cleopatra was just ten years old, her father paid the leaders of Rome (Pompey, Caesar, and Crassus) six thousand talents of gold, which roughly equaled Egypt's entire revenue for one year. In exchange for money, Rome agreed to support Ptolemy XII against any rebellion growing within his country.

While attaining Roman support was vital to Ptolemy XII remaining on the throne, he paid a heavy cost for it. For one, to keep his subjects from having to pay the bribe to Rome at one time, he borrowed the money from a Roman moneylender and planned to spread the new taxes over several years to repay the loan. The added interest of the loan only added to the burden. His subjects were hurt even more by the new taxes.

Second, Ptolemy XII lost what little respect he had from his subjects after his deal. They saw him as a Roman puppet. One year after Ptolemy XII paid the bribe, a Roman general seized the Egyptian island of Cyprus, which was ruled by Ptolemy XII's brother. Rather than face the humiliation of dethronement, Cleopatra's uncle committed suicide. Her father did nothing about it, which incited more anger among his subjects. In light of this, Ptolemy XII took Cleopatra and fled to Rome, fearing that it was unsafe to stay in Egypt.

Ptolemy XII's oldest daughter, Cleopatra VI, used her father's exile as an opportunity to seize the throne, but she was soon murdered by her sister Berenice, who ruled with her husband. While in power, Berenice plotted to have her father killed. She sent messengers to Rome asking for her father's immediate return to Egypt.

In response, Ptolemy XII offered the Roman government ten thousand talents in return for their support in attacking his daughter Berenice and restoring him to the throne. The Roman government agreed, and Berenice was quickly captured and then executed.

INTERPRETATION

The world Cleopatra lived in was truly one of contrasts: On the one hand, it was rich and filled with culture, luxury, and promise; but on the other hand, it was very volatile, uncertain, and dangerous. Both external factors (i.e., The Roman government, civil unrest, and corruption in the government) and internal factors (i.e., family feuding, infighting, and scheming courtiers) played a major role in shaping Cleopatra's life, and the way she would later try to govern her kingdom.

Multiple external and internal factors also currently shape public education and the way teachers perform their duties within their classrooms. Although some factors may be specific to a particular state or region of the country, some factors are prevalent in all school districts across the United States. Such factors permeate the public educational landscape, and they have significant bearing on what is taught inside classrooms across America. The following are external and internal factors that nearly all public schoolteachers in America have in common.

External Factors

The first external factor that adversely affects all public schoolteachers is the current debate surrounding public education reform. America's public educational system is currently undergoing tremendous change. Lawmakers, politicians, and scholars are all debating how to reform public education. These debates are sparked primarily by ballooning financial costs and low student achievement.

During the 1960s through the 1980s, America's public educational system was ranked among the highest in the world compared with other industrialized nations. This changed as the 1990s rolled in. America's top students started to show gradual declines in math and science. According to Pearson, a global education reporting firm, American students are currently ranked seventeenth worldwide among modern nations (Graziano, 2005). Because of America's global educational decline, politicians and corporate leaders are trying to reform public education—often without input from practitioners working in the field. This has created tension and division between those who set educational policies and those who implement them.

The second external factor comes by way of the No Child Left Behind Act (NCLB), passed in 2000 by former president George W. Bush. This federal legislation requires all public school districts receiving federal money to show adequate yearly academic progress based on specific criteria. School districts that do not show yearly progress lose some, if not all, of the federal money they receive under the Title I Act. This piece of legislation also helped to usher in the standards-based movement and the use of standardized testing as the primary tool for measuring annual student achievement. Many public schoolteachers believe that the overemphasis placed on standardized testing has caused them to "teach to the test" instead of teaching according to the needs and deficiencies of their students.

The third external factor involves the intense scrutiny from the media. Negative stories published by various media outlets about failing public schools have become the norm rather than the exception. Such stories help to shape opinions about public education, and change the types of support public schools receive from their communities. The brunt of this criticism typically falls on teachers.

In many ways, the media has made public schoolteachers the sacrificial lambs for nearly every problem in our society. The negative stories from the media often give people the impression that everything wrong with American society is a result of ineffective public schools. In reality, the exact opposite is true: Ineffective public schools are often created by the deterioration of many American communities—which is the fourth external factor adversely affecting public schoolteachers.

The deterioration of large metropolitan communities is arguably the most detrimental external factor affecting public education today. Many families and communities in America are still disproportionately affected by poverty. These communities are not only poor and lacking resources, but are also plagued by violence, drugs and alcoholism, gangs, unemployment, substandard housing and healthcare, and a host of other socioeconomic problems. Many of the same issues that adversely affect poverty-stricken communities also negatively affect the schools that serve the people living in such communities, making the teaching and learning process even more challenging.

Internal Factors

Aside from the aforementioned external factors associated with America's drop in worldwide educational rankings, several internal factors detract from the work that teachers try to accomplish with students. Such adverse factors directly affect public schoolteachers, and have a significant effect on what happens within their respective classrooms. Again, such internal factors are indicative of the school district and the region of the country where the school district is located. Some of the internal factors are so imposing that they can affect a teacher's ability to remain employed.

For example, US public schools hire a little over 200,000 new teachers every year to start the first day of class, but more than 22,000 quit by the end of the school year (Graziano, 2005). The average teacher yearly turnover rate is about 30 percent nationally (Kain, 2011). The problem is more acute in the nation's high-minority, high-poverty, and low-performing urban school districts where the teacher turnover rate is an alarming 46 percent (Kain, 2011). Most teachers who leave the teaching profession do so after only three to five years of service (Kain, 2011).

Many reasons contribute to why teachers leave the profession early, but one reason stands out. According to a 2009 survey conducted by the National Center for Education Statistics, the number one reason why teachers leave the profession early is because of the pressure they receive from the demands associated with standardized testing. As mentioned previously, the increased use of standardized testing as the primary measurement of student achievement has greatly affected the teaching profession.

Some school districts have essentially turned their schools into test factories. They not only administer district-wide assessments to students every six to eight weeks, they also require teachers to use more guided practice, direct instruction techniques, memorization, and use the standardized test format as their sole curriculum guide. Other school districts have reduced the amount of time students receive during recess, or they have eliminated arts programs and elective courses, to give students more time to work on test-taking skills and materials.

A large number of school districts are now tinkering with the idea of linking students' performance on standardized tests to a teacher's overall performance evaluation. Low student test scores could mean an ineffective rating for the teacher on his or her formal evaluation, which could eventually lead to termination of employment. Other school districts have also implemented pay-for-performance incentives that give teachers substantial bonuses when their students perform well on standardized tests. This has caused some school officials and personnel to behave unethically by cheating. Several districts across the country have erased students' incorrect answers and bubbled in the correct answers to attain the monetary bonuses at the end of the school year. Their main focus became improving test scores instead of improving students' overall achievement.

Many teachers believe that the byproduct of the pressure felt from standardized testing is the creation of school administrators who are often nonresponsive and out of touch with the actual needs of teachers (Kain, 2011). Receiving assistance with issues such as disruptive students and disgruntled parents and obtaining quality feedback and professional development rank among teachers' top complaints about school administrators.

Without a doubt, this is a very volatile and uncertain period in American public education. The aforementioned factors all have political, social, and economic overtones. These are just a few of the major issues that make up the public educational landscape today. Although the factors and circumstances affecting teachers are not life-threatening like those surrounding Cleopatra, they still have significant bearing on the teaching profession, student achievement, and American society as a whole.

The aforementioned factors are just a few of the major issues that public schoolteachers face on a yearly basis—and there are definitely a lot more. Some of the other factors include—but are not limited to—student discipline, parental involvement (or lack thereof), school culture, staff morale, budget reductions that lead to layoffs, and the lack of recognition. With all of the intense pressure created by such sources, it appears that teachers are fighting an uphill battle that seems impossible to win.

Even though the challenges faced by today's public schoolteachers are daunting, there is still hope. Public schoolteachers truly have the capacity to lead the revolution of change instead of playing the role of passive victims. They have the ability to take most of the power out of the hands of school administrators, politicians, businessmen, and law makers, and put it where it truly belongs: back in the hands of those who work directly with students—the practitioners.

America's public educational system is at a crossroads. It will either continue to fall behind, or it will elevate to a higher level and possibly regain the dominance it once had. To achieve the highest levels possible for students, public schoolteachers not only need a keen understanding of all the factors affecting their work, they also need to be skilled in the art of student engagement. Every aspect of a teacher's job is connected to his or her ability to engage students effectively within the classroom.

According to Taylor and Parsons (2011) the following are evident when students are engaged in their lessons and actively participating in the learning process:

- Student engagement occurs when students make a psychological investment in their learning.
- Students are fully emerged in the learning process, which will allow them to later take what they've learned and incorporate it in their lives.
- Students are engaged when they are involved in their work, persist despite challenges and obstacles, and take visible delight in accomplishing their work.
- The byproduct of student engagement is increased levels of student achievement.
- Students have a willingness, need, desire, and compulsion to participate and be successful in the learning process, promoting higher-level thinking for enduring understanding.

Student engagement will not only elevate classroom instruction and heighten students' learning experiences, it will also be one of the greatest indicators that will insulate teachers from the internal and external factors that adversely affect their work (Taylor & Parsons, 2011). Teachers who are skilled at engaging students will undoubtedly have the most success. They will not have to worry about threats associated with the aforementioned factors because their students will show academic growth from one year to the next.

KEYS TO TEACHING

There is no doubt that public schoolteachers face many factors that affect their daily work. Such factors also contribute to the reasons why teachers are leaving the profession at such alarming rates. If a teacher's ability to engage students will help to insulate him or her against the various factors adversely affecting the work, then the actions to attain the highest levels of engagement should be driven by a teacher's core values and beliefs about education. Without a solid grounding in one's core values and beliefs about education, public schoolteachers will quickly become lost, frustrated, unwilling, or unable to remain in the profession. A teacher's core values and beliefs about education must be cemented before stepping inside any classroom to teach.

The current nature of public education can make it easy for teachers to become sidetracked and discombobulated. The bureaucracy, politics, and dynamics of most public school systems (especially large school districts that serve a high concentration of students of low socioeconomic status) are enough to test the resolve of any sincere education professional. This is part of the reason why so many teachers leave the profession within the first five years of their careers. In such volatile times, teachers truly need something solid to stand on and something meaningful to stand for. In times of frustration and self-doubt, that "something" is none other than the principles they value as true education professionals. Such sacred jewels stem from a teacher's core beliefs about education.

A teacher's core beliefs about education help provide answers to the following questions: Who are you, and what are your professional goals as an educator? What do you value the most about teaching and learning, and how will you impart that to your students? How will your work as a teacher be used to empower students? How can you get students to think critically about the world around them? In what ways would you like your students to grow? How will you work to maximize instruction? What is the purpose of the curriculum, and how will you use it to advance student learning? Do you bring any personal biases or prejudices to the classroom? If so, what will you do to prevent yourself from including your biases and prejudices within the classroom? Which of your values and beliefs about teaching and learning are nonnegotiable? How do you want others to view you as a teaching professional? What kind of educator do you want to be, and how will you personally help represent the profession? How can you model equity and justice in your classroom?

The answers to the aforementioned questions should strike at the core of any teacher's belief system about education, and cause one to reflect on the primary reasons why he or she entered the profession in the first place. These questions will also cause a teacher to look critically at him- or herself to identify any personal biases and prejudices that could interfere in work with students. Understand: Although a teacher's personal beliefs on politics, religion, orientation, and other life experiences make up who he or she is as an individual, such personal views and opinions should never interfere in the educational process involving students. Allowing them to do so could introduce additional factors into the classroom that could be harmful to students or be detrimental to the overall teaching and learning process.

Your core values and beliefs about education are connected to who you are (or aspire to be) as a teaching professional. Such beliefs about education will be a teacher's anchor when times become difficult or challenging: Such beliefs will also serve as the fuel a teacher needs to keep going when students are uncooperative, when parents are disgruntled, when school administrators are unsupportive, and when morale is low. Understand: A teacher's core values and beliefs can serve as the driving force behind everything he or she does as an education professional. Take Cleopatra as an example: She knew what kind of queen she wanted to be from the start and the type of kingdom she wanted to govern. Her core beliefs were the driving force behind all of her actions. She set the bar high for herself, and she demanded that others— including the great Roman Empire—respect and treat her the same way. She was in tune with her core values and beliefs, which served as the passion behind her actions.

Public schoolteachers need to operate in a similar fashion. They need to be in touch with their passions and genuine beliefs about teaching and learning, and let those beliefs guide their actions and decisions. Such beliefs will be the catalyst that pushes teachers to master their content areas, create interesting lessons, stay abreast of best practices and pedagogies, maintain open lines of communication with parents, continue working when interdistrict systems are flawed, and be in tune with the needs of their respective students.

All teachers must have their own high standards of excellence—standards they are not willing to diminish for any one or any reason. Teachers who don't know who they are professionally will have a difficult time working and collaborating with others within today's volatile public school climate. They will end up assuming roles and taking on characteristics not of their own making, and not aligned with their professional DNA.

Being an effective public schoolteacher in today's climate is half about what you do; the other half is about who you are as a professional. The most effective teachers are those who have a keen understanding of their core values, principles, and beliefs about education. Depending on the type of school district a teacher is working in, such values and beliefs could be the only thing that keeps the teacher from giving up completely.

In addition, public schoolteachers should never become complacent, accept failure, or settle for subpar performance from themselves or their students. In a profession that's ever-changing, multifaceted, and becoming increasingly uncertain, public schoolteachers have to be confident in themselves and relentless in their pursuit of excellence. All public schoolteachers have a choice: They can stand by and continue with the status quo or they can do what Cleopatra did and take charge of their own destinies. My hope is that after reading this book, all teachers will choose the latter.

SUMMARY POINTS

- External and internal factors currently shape public education and the way teachers perform their duties within the classroom.
- Public schools are receiving intense scrutiny from the media.
- The average teacher attrition rate in America is about 30 percent.
- Student engagement is the cornerstone for effective teaching.
- A public schoolteacher's personal biases about religion, politics, sexual orientation, and race have no place in the teaching and learning process.
- Know yourself and stick to your core values and beliefs about teaching and learning.

2

RULE I

Know Your Students

To truly reach students and achieve significant academic growth, teachers must first take time to really get to know their students academically as well as personally. Having a complete understanding of their students not only helps build positive relationships, but also gives teachers insight on how to resolve issues associated with students' overall educational and development needs.

ORIENTATION[1]

In 51 BC, Cleopatra's father died. Shortly before his death, he named Cleopatra and her younger brother Ptolemy XIII, who was only ten at the time, as his joint successors from among his four remaining children. This was not acceptable to Cleopatra or her younger siblings (Ptolemy XIII, Arsinoe, and Ptolemy XIV). They all wanted more power. As was the custom of royal Egyptian families at that time, the chosen children had to marry each other and rule the kingdom as husband and wife. Cleopatra and her brother did marry, but that was the extent of their union.

---

1. The text in this section is a paraphrased narrative derived from facts presented by Roller (2010), Tyldesley (2008), Flamarion (1993), and Sapet (2007).

At the time of her father's death, Cleopatra was eighteen. Even at such a young age, she showed leadership qualities and was already adored by her subjects. She was able to connect with the Egyptian people in ways that her father and brother were unable to. As a young queen she carried out her duties and looked after the people absent of her coruling husband-brother. This upset her brother's advisers and prompted them to conspire against her.

Ptolemy XIII's chief advisers, Pothinus, a eunuch, and Achillas, head general of the Egyptian army, were Cleopatra's main enemies. Both of them wanted to dethrone Cleopatra and make her husband-brother the sole ruler. They began teaching the young Ptolemy XIII to hate and envy his wife-sister, which he did.

In 49 BC, Cleopatra fled from the capital city of Alexandria to Syria. Not much is known about why she departed, but it was probably from rumors of plots against her from Ptolemy XIII's camp. She arrived in Syria with a small band of loyal followers and began to organize support against her brother. She used her knowledge of Hebrew and Arabic to communicate with local leaders. Determined and crafty, she managed to build a small army in hopes of turning back to Alexandria to reclaim her throne.

Meanwhile, Ptolemy XIII's advisers used the large Egyptian army to block the coastal roads and thwart any attempt Cleopatra made to return to Alexandria. Sensing her army was no match for her brother's, Cleopatra waited to stage her attack. She stayed in Syria a little over three years. While Cleopatra and her brother were preparing to lock horns, another power struggle was taking place in Rome.

Julius Caesar and Gnaeus Pompey were battling for control of Rome. Pompey, who was losing the power struggle, fled to his allies in Italy. While in Italy, he asked for help from Egypt. He asked for ships, grain, and men to help him defeat Caesar. Ptolemy's chief adviser, Pothinus, who was really ruling Egypt at the time, obliged Pompey's requests. Despite Egypt's support, Pompey was still defeated by Caesar, whose legions were superior and more disciplined.

After losing a battle against Caesar in Northern Greece, Pompey fled to Egypt to ask Ptolemy to finance a future mission against Caesar. Pompey anticipated a friendly welcoming into Egypt, but Pothinus viewed Pompey as a loser in the Roman struggle and he didn't think his young king should be sided with a loser. In an attempt to win Caesar's support, Pothinus plotted to murder Pompey. On September 28, 48 BC, Ptolemy lured Pompey into Egypt under the pretense that he would support Pompey. Upon entering the seaport, Pompey was stabbed to death by Egyptian conspirators. His head was severed and was later presented to Caesar as a gift.

Unaware that Pompey was already dead, Caesar marched into Egypt in pursuit of him. Caesar's goal was to capture Pompey and collect the long overdue debts the Egyptian government owed Rome to pay his soldiers. He arrived in Egypt with four ships and ten thousand soldiers four days after Pompey's death.

Ptolemy and his advisers presented Pompey's severed head as a token of their friendship to Rome, but to their surprise Caesar became visibly upset. He didn't like the undignified way the former Roman general was treated in death. Caesar ordered the execution of Pompey's murderers. For this he remained in Alexandria, occupying the royal palace and raiding the Egyptian treasury. Caesar also demanded to see both Ptolemy and Cleopatra together to put an end to their infighting.

Ptolemy's advisers were uncomfortable with Caesar's presence, and they were not interested in having him play peacemaker. They anticipated that Caesar would leave Egypt quickly. When he didn't leave as they hoped, they began spreading anti-Roman rhetoric across Egypt and plotted to kill Caesar. In the meantime, the Egyptian army was still stationed at all of the entries, and they were ordered to kill Cleopatra on sight.

Unlike her brother, Cleopatra knew she didn't have a chance of fighting against Rome. She wanted to negotiate with Caesar, but Ptolemy's army stood between her and Alexandria. To reach Caesar, she came up with a daring plan to sneak into the royal palace. One night, Cleopatra, accompanied by a Syrian ally, entered the Egyptian harbor by way of a small boat. Upon docking, the Syrian wrapped Cleopatra up in a thick piece of carpet, picked her up, and carried her past the Egyptian soldiers and palace guards. He took her directly into Caesar's chambers. The carpet was unfurled at Caesar's feet, and the young queen surprisingly tumbled before him.

This dangerous gambit paid off. Caesar was impressed by her bravery. He knew it took guts to successfully pull off such a stunt. That entire evening, and throughout that night, the two shared each other's company. Caesar was enchanted by her intelligence, charm, beauty, and wit. At age twenty-one, she was very alluring to the fifty-two-year-old Caesar. Shrewd and intelligent, she spoke to Caesar in his native tongue, and she impressed him with her knowledge of the arts, culture, scholarship, and military strategy. Caesar was spellbound by Cleopatra. With physical, political, and mental attraction between them, the two became lovers that same night.

The next day, Caesar invited Ptolemy, now thirteen, to his chambers. Ptolemy was shocked to see his sister Cleopatra by Caesar's side; she had outmaneuvered him. Ptolemy and his advisers were even more dismayed that Caesar had taken her side instead of theirs.

INTERPRETATION

Many historians believe Cleopatra had such an intense effect on Caesar simply because he was a middle-age man while she was a young, vibrant woman in the prime of her life. In reality, that is far from the truth. Caesar was known as being somewhat of a lady's man in his own right. His wealth, fame, and power afforded him the luxury of having the finest women Rome had to offer. His affairs with wives of various members of the senate and several of the top aristocrats in Rome are documented. He was even rumored to have had an affair with the wife of his rival, Pompey.

Caesar was smitten by Cleopatra because she had intimate knowledge about him, which she used to her advantage. When Cleopatra was young and fleeing from Egypt with her father, she lived in Rome for several years. During that time she received an early education in Roman society. She learned of their history, culture, social norms, and taboos. Cleopatra also learned what Romans valued and what they detested.

Later as an adult and coruler of Egypt, she quickly understood that she needed Rome as an ally to stay in power. Cleopatra closely monitored Rome's political landscape to see which way the pendulum of power would swing. Once she discovered that Caesar's stock had risen, she gathered whatever information she could about him. For example, she knew that Caesar was an ambitious man who loved war and politics. In fact, he often openly compared himself to Alexander the Great. He was also a brilliant writer, politician, and orator. He was admired by

Romans for his intellect, courage in battle, and for his generosity toward his soldiers.

Cleopatra also learned about an incident that happened in Caesar's life when he was in his mid-twenties. One day while Caesar was at sea, he and his crew members were captured by pirates. This was a potentially dangerous situation, but Caesar remained under control and successfully negotiated with the pirates. After he was set free, he came back with several ships, captured the same pirates, and annihilated them all. This act won Caesar great fame and respect throughout Rome.

The information she obtained on Caesar was enough to create a strategic plan. When the two finally had a chance to meet face to face, it was as if Caesar was meeting his soul mate. She appealed to his interests and desires, making him feel comfortable and relaxed in her presence. She was charming, intellectual, and cunning—all the characteristics Caesar admired.

Several years later, she also used the same strategy on Mark Antony. Unlike Caesar who favored intellectual stimuli, Antony loved physical pleasures. He was considered to be a handsome man who enjoyed keeping his body in top shape. It was said that he used to wear his togas low to show off his physique. He also loved to tell dirty jokes, host lavish parties, and enjoy his fill of wine. To gain his attention and political backing, Cleopatra simply appealed to his unique set of interests. During the time Cleopatra and Antony spent together, she showered him with lavish banquettes, fine linen, and silk clothing, and hosted wild parties in his honor. She used what she knew about him to build a connection and influence his behavior.

Cleopatra's charm was not in her seductive powers, but instead was her ability to be in tune with the needs and sensitivities of other people. She was aware of people's differences and what made them unique as individuals. Knowing her targets well—their attitudes, nuances, strengths, weaknesses, desires, and personal interests—gave Cleopatra immense power.

KEYS TO TEACHING

Learning is a complex process with many interacting variables that influence outcomes for students. If one variable is missing, or if one is too dominant, it could have great implications for students' ability to learn and a teacher's ability to teach.

Public schoolteachers must be aware of all the factors that play a role in their students' ability to learn. The only way to do this is for teachers to have a thorough understanding of their students. Just like Cleopatra made an effort to be in touch with the people of her kingdom, public schoolteachers also have an urgent need to be in tune with the sensitivities and nuances of their students, and all the variables that will affect learning outcomes.

In today's tough educational climate, teachers must make genuine connections with students to reach them. According to Weiner (2003) teachers need knowledge of what students' lives are like outside of school to make connections, personal and intellectual, between school learning and lived experiences. In doing so, teachers will be able to build more significant relationships with students, which is the foundation for effective teaching practice (Weiner, 2003).

Teachers must expand their knowledge about their student population, and attain as much information about them as possible. Doing so will give teachers an understanding of how students view the world around them; more importantly, it will inform teachers of how they can work to expand that view. To acquire such knowledge takes a lot of diligence on the part of a teacher.

Because students have unique experiences outside of school, many students present different barriers to the teaching and learning process. Such barriers could include a dysfunctional home environment, lack of parental support, low self-esteem, unstable living arrangements, learning disabilities, or various forms of neglect and abuse, just to name a few. Depending on the severity of their experiences, some students will not easily participate, share, collaborate, respond, or take educational risks in a classroom setting.

Many students who fall in this category misbehave, become truant, or completely shut down to mask their deficiencies. Others are guarded and defensive out of fear of failure, being hurt or misled, or being embarrassed in front of their peers. Some students don't take school or their education seriously. They view their time in school primarily as a means to socialize with their peers; therefore, it is hard to get them to respond to anything outside the social realm of their individual school experiences. The only way to pierce through such barriers, and gain access to student information that will aide in the learning process, is for teachers to establish trust and rapport with their students. This is the first step in trying to effectively engage students and deliver quality instruction.

Many teachers are still under the erroneous impression that they must act in an authoritative fashion to take control of their classrooms, gain students' compliance, and deliver quality instruction. Some teachers still believe they shouldn't smile until the month of December. This notion is as much false as it is ineffective at helping teachers build rapport with students and gain valuable information that can be useful during the teaching and learning process. Acting too authoritative, especially in the beginning, will turn the majority of students off: It will make students feel alienated and cause them to resist the teacher and possibly the concepts being taught. The resistance will ultimately lead to students rejecting classroom norms and expectations. Having thorough knowledge about students is a teacher's gateway toward connecting with them, and learning how to best serve their academic needs.

This knowledge extends beyond knowing what is inside students' cumulative folder in the main office, grade point averages, or their latest scores on standardized tests. It means having access to information about the students' lives outside school. This is instrumental because in most cases the circumstances and events of a child's life outside school can either enhance or hinder the child's academic development inside school.

Many public schoolteachers make the mistake of trying to attend to a student's academic needs without checking on the social-emotional needs first. This mentality is mainly fostered by pressure teachers experience to improve standardized test scores. This type of pressure has caused public schoolteachers to become more content oriented and less concerned about the overall developmental needs of students. The humanistic side of teaching and learning has either taken a backseat or has been ignored in many classrooms. I'm not saying that the academic side of teaching and learning is less important than the social-emotional aspect, but there has to be a balance—and one side (the social-emotional) should go before the other (academic).

Teachers who are able to function as an intermediary between the outer classroom variables and the students will have tremendous suc-

cess. Failure to acquire intimate knowledge about students before trying to deliver instruction is like a doctor trying to treat a patient without
first diagnosing the patient's symptoms; it just doesn't make sense.

The Most Useful Student Information

Too many teachers come into public education with what I call the
"save the children" mentality. They hear stories, read articles and statistics, or watch news reports and documentaries about how troubled
public schools are, and it prompts them to try to take action. There is
nothing wrong with people wanting to make a difference in the lives of
students, but there is one element working against them: These educators often enter classrooms with their own perceptions and precon-
ceived notions about what public school students need, and then they
try to resolve the problems they encounter based on their own understanding.

Often the perception of what students (and their families) need, the
resources provided to them, and the reality of what they actually should
have are not aligned because no one ever inquires to find out how
students perceive themselves and the world around them. The truth of
the matter is that teachers will not be able to effectively deal with the
content and other academic paradigms until they are able to make
genuine connections with students. Such connections will not be possible until teachers make a conscious effort to really learn about their
students.

To gain knowledge about students that will be useful inside the
classroom, teachers need to gather three types of information: global,
local, and individual. Gathering such information will not only help
teachers gain a thorough understanding of their students, but it will also
assist with creating positive connections that will enhance the teaching
and learning process and produce positive academic outcomes.

Global information consists of student information that is common
to every school within the entire school district. This will give teachers
an expanded view of the school district's student population. This includes but is not limited to learning student demographics, ethnic backgrounds, languages, percentage of students on free and reduced lunch,
past and most current academic performance on standardized tests,
frequency of suspensions and expulsions, graduation rates, percentage

identified as special needs or English language learners, and the soci-oeconomic status of students. Much of this information can usually be found on any school district's website.

Teachers can also gather such information by conversing with indi-viduals working at the central office level who gather and use such information on a regular basis. They should communicate with individ-uals up and down the chain of command within the school district, listening and observing. Even though all of the information from such interactions may not be useful, it still will help to expand a teacher's view of the school district and give a global perspective of the student population as a whole.

Local information has two distinct parts: The first part pertains to the actual school where the teacher has been assigned to work, and the second part deals with the community (or communities) where the students live. Local information about a teacher's particular school is similar to global information except that it is more concentrated and specific to the actual place where the teacher works.

The most useful information about a school includes information about student achievement, attendance, student discipline, suspension rates, ethnic background and language, the number on free and re-duced lunch, percentage with special needs, and the average class size, just to name a few. It can also include items associated with the school's culture such as ceremonies and celebrations, student events, special programs, accepted norms and practices, teacher morale, heroes and heroines, and information about the school's parent-teacher association.

The second half of local information deals with the community where students live. Typically, this information is about the same com-munity where the school is located, but that's not always the case. If students live in a community located outside of the one where the school is located, then teachers should gather information on the school and on the students' home community. Important community informa-tion includes data associated with housing, employment rates, crime statistics, family structures, events and festivals, community norms and beliefs, religious affiliations, and the ethnic backgrounds and languages of the residents to name a few.

Most of the aforementioned items pertaining to local information are all public record, which can be found on most city, county, or state websites. But to really understand local information, teachers have to actually visit the community (or communities) where their students live. Local libraries, churches, or grocery stores are excellent for meeting people who live in the community, and for acquiring further understanding of the school where the teacher works. It would also help to visit the community during a festival or other special event, or attend a town hall meeting. Visiting the community yourself is helpful for filtering through information obtained from the Internet and from conversations, which might be tainted or biased depending on whom you talk to.

Teachers must take in as much local information as possible with their own eyes without putting any restrictions on or drawing any barriers to their social interactions with people within the community. When gathering local information, teachers should deliberately go places that are typically beyond the usual circle for teachers. This will help teachers make connections and help them understand the environment where the students actually come from.

Global and local student information will help teachers develop a picture of the students prior to the first day of class, but teachers will benefit the most when they combine global and local information with individual information. Individual information pertains directly to the students listed on the teacher's class rosters. These are the students a teacher will see and work with each day throughout the school year.

Unlike the other sources of information that can be obtained before teachers have a chance to actually meet their students, teachers gather individual information starting on the first day of class and continuing throughout the school year. This information takes a little more time because there is usually only one teacher serving many students within the classroom. Therefore, teachers should take their time and work to develop a keen understanding about each student within their class or classes. Furthermore, global and local information may not change much from year to year, but teachers will receive different students at the beginning of each school year; therefore, teachers must continually work to gain individual information with each set of new students.

Some of the most useful student information includes but is not limited to a student's temperament, work ethic, behavior patterns, cognitive ability, academic strengths and deficiencies, nonacademic interests, and peer relations. Although the majority of information must be gathered gradually as the school year progress, teachers can collect it in a variety of ways, including through conversations with parents, caregivers, and colleagues who might have history with the students. But the most effective way to gather student information is through direct inter-personal dialogue, observations, and interactions with students in the classroom.

Understand: Information from second- and third-party sources can be useful, but they should not be the primary means for learning about students. Teachers need to see, listen, and communicate with students first hand. They need to establish their own relationships with students, and determine what their needs are without any filters from other sources. This can only be done through direct, ongoing interactions.

During the first few days of school, teachers should spend significant time with ice-breakers, interest surveys, and fun activities that help build rapport. This will help make teachers seem more likable and friendly in the eyes of their students. During this time, students will reveal their personal interests, feelings, opinions, hobbies, nicknames, and other characteristics about themselves. They will also reveal aspects of their personality. This is also the time when teachers have the oppor-tunity to make connections and emphasize the things they have in com-mon with their students.

For example, one student may reveal that she has a pet dog; another student might be into sports, while others might have musical or artistic interests. Teachers could use such information to make connections from aspects of their own lives. Even if no commonalities appear in the beginning, the teacher can use examples from other people, or tell stories that could resonate with students based on the information the students have shared.

When I was a classroom teacher, I had the opportunity of teaching in the same high school that I once attended. As a child, I lived in the same community where my students lived, and had many similar expe-riences. These similarities served as powerful mechanisms for connect-ing with my students. The stories I told, the people I knew, and the places I described connected with my students on many levels.

I also used several of my most current experiences to connect with my students. For example, I learned that many of my students were interested in music, so I told them about my experiences with assisting a personal friend with pursuing his music career. I shared the things I knew about recording, CD manufacturing, booking shows, and legal contracts. Sharing such information allowed me to connect with my students in a genuine way—I was even able to incorporate some of their topics of interest into a few of my lessons.

According to Lieberman (2000) the most important factor in forming any kind of bond with someone is to first get the person to like you. You don't get a person to like you by making a display of your differences; instead, you must stress the things that are similar (Lieberman, 2000). This applies to the student-teacher relationship as well. I'm not referring to a buddy- or peer-type relationship, because that would be detrimental to the teaching and learning process; rather, the teacher should cultivate the kind of connection that fosters mutual respect between a student and a school official. Students who like their teachers become students who trust their teachers. If students trust their teachers, they will be willing to take academic risks in the classroom, expose their areas of deficiency, and be receptive to accepting help. Once the areas of weakness have been discovered by the teacher, and the student is receptive to assistance, then the teacher can create strategic plans for resolving such issues.

Getting people to like her was a strategy Cleopatra often used to her advantage. When she was first named coruler with her brother Ptolemy, one of the first things she did was to make a connection with the people of Egypt. The young Cleopatra, being only eighteen at the time, took on the persona of Isis, one of the most popular Egyptian deities. While in public, she adorned herself with garments and jewelry that made her resemble the Egyptian deity.

All of the Ptolemies were of Greek descent, but Cleopatra knew that making a show of her Greek heritage wasn't the way to connect with her Egyptian subjects. She spoke using the Egyptian language, and she participated in nearly all of the annual Egyptian festivals and ceremonies celebrated during that time. Because of this, the people of Egypt adored her. She made a sharp contrast to her brother and coruler who kept distance between himself and the people of Egypt. He never attempted to win the people over in any way.

One strategy I used when I was a teacher was to incorporate various aspects from the students' community into the classroom. For example, the supply closet was named "Mama Bell's" after a popular candy store located in the students' neighborhood. The bookshelf was called "Heavies" after a popular restaurant in their community. Also, I often referred to my classroom as the "Hub" after the recreation center located near the school. All of my students knew of these places within their community, and using such names in class allowed my students to make connections with my classroom in a genuine way.

On the surface these things may appear to be insignificant or trivial. Their significance lies in showing that the teacher values things that are valuable to students, which allows for a deeper connection between the students and the teacher. Incorporating aspects from the students' world into the classroom also creates a sense of belonging, which connects them to the school's culture in a positive way and enhances the students' overall educational experience.

Another powerful way for teachers to show commonality with students is to incorporate some of the students' terminology and ways of speaking into the classroom. Using certain terms and gestures is a way to show similarity and to make yourself likable (Lieberman, 2000). Teachers can not only use their understanding of such terms to build rapport with students, but doing so also helps teachers communicate more effectively, making teachers appear more relatable in their students' eyes.

Warning: This technique should be used sparingly, and only with teachers who have established a strong rapport and developed a long history with students. I say this because teachers never want to make themselves look immature or be viewed as a student's peer by talking in the same manner and acting exactly like the student population. If language is used in the wrong way, it could have an adverse effect and diminish the students' respect for the teacher. This technique is best used as a pathway to help students understand higher-order vocabulary and phrases as they relate to lessons or concepts taught in class, or to show students how to speak grammatically.

For example, when I was a teacher, I frequently heard students use words such as *chillin*, *skep*, *salty*, *faded*, *thirsty*, and *flexin* in their daily speech. I learned that when someone is *chillin*, they are relaxing or trying to have a good time. If someone is *skep*, they are untrustworthy and should be watched closely. To be *salty* means that you are mad about something, or disappointed that a situation didn't go your way. A person who is *faded* is drunk or high on drugs. Being *thirsty* means that a person is overzealous in a negative way or motivated for the wrong reasons. When someone is *flexin*, they are showing off or trying to display their dominance.

Many of my students used such terminology because those were the words that were used by people in their communities and households. Also, many of my students had limited vocabularies; they didn't have any other words to use when expressing themselves. Having a keen understanding of the terminology that students used allowed me to bridge the gap between language that they used in their world, and the academic language they needed to be successful in school and beyond.

For example, when teaching I would strategically use a word like *perpetrator* in the same context as the students (which to them meant a fraud or a fake). Then I would immediately follow it up by using a more secular word like *charlatan*. Doing so helped students make connections with other words. Over time, students began to incorporate the new words into their vocabularies. I was also able to use certain words from the students' vernacular to increase their understanding of a particular concept.

For example, I sometimes noticed students having trouble comprehending something after I explained the topic using formal words and definitions. I would then explain the particular concept again using the terminology students were familiar with. This increased their understanding and mastery. Once they were able to catch on, I went back to the formal terms and definitions. Today's public school students also have specific terminology they use on a daily basis. Having a keen understanding of this terminology can be the gateway for public school-teachers to establish rapport and increase students' understanding of vocabulary and key concepts.

Furthermore, when teachers take time to establish rapport with students at the beginning, and continue such efforts throughout the course of a calendar school year, their efforts will eventually pay off. This is true because the connections created between students and their teachers will decrease some (if not all) of the early resistance teachers usually encounter from students. The connections will also allow a student to let their guards down, which also leads to establishing trust. Once trust has been established, students will be susceptible to the teacher's rules and expectations for learning and acceptable behavior.

Second, when students encounter an academic problem, they will be more likely to divulge their issues, providing that the issues are not already apparent to the teacher. For example, during my teaching career I encountered a student with a very peculiar situation. He had the cognitive ability to succeed academically, but his grades suffered. The biggest reasons for his poor grades were his lack of homework and his attendance issues.

This particular student was often tardy to my first-period class. I pulled the student aside one day and asked him about his lack of homework and tardiness. It turned out that the student held a part-time job to help his single mother pay bills and maintain their household expenses. After he got off work, he had to catch a bus to pick up his three younger siblings from the babysitter, and get on another bus to get home. Once home he had to prepare dinner for himself and his siblings, do a variety of chores around the house, and prepare for the next day before going to sleep. His mother did not usually arrive home from work until after 11:00 p.m. And if his chores were not done to his mother's satisfaction, she would wake him up at night and make him do them again.

It's unfortunate, but this young man didn't have time to do homework for me or any other teacher on a consistent basis. His schedule also helped explain why he was often late to school in the morning, because he often overslept or was late for some reason associated with his home environment. Knowing this information allowed me to assist this student in ways that were beneficial for him and his current circumstances. If I wasn't able to establish some level of trust and rapport with the student in the beginning, he probably wouldn't have shared such intimate details of his home life after only knowing me for such a short time. It is also very likely that if I had not received information as to why the student was having trouble, it could have possibly led to the student receiving a failing grade for my class because of his excessive tardiness and lack of homework completion.

I have countless other examples where my rapport-building efforts led to students sharing details about their home life or personal situations, which gave me more insight on how to instruct them. In nearly every situation, I was either able to assist them with the resources they needed to be successful, or I was able to find someone in the school building or community who could assist them if I wasn't able to.

In gaining knowledge about students, it is a strong possibility that teachers will inadvertently become privy to information of a personal nature (e.g., divorced parents, homelessness, negligent parents, prior hurts and abuses, financial troubles, illnesses, lacking one or more basic needs, etc.). After being exposed to such information—whether from a student, parent, or any second-hand source—teachers must always be mindful of the students' feelings and of their confidentiality. Under no circumstances should a teacher gossip or indiscriminately share a student's private personal information with another student, adult, or colleague without permission.

It may not be the student's desire to share such information with another person, and there is no way to control how the other person will use such information or with whom they might share it. If students want their private information to get out, then let them be the ones to spread it. The only exception to this rule is if the teacher becomes privy to information that a student or someone else is in physical or mental danger. In such cases, the teacher should inform the head school official or contact the proper authorities.

More importantly, teachers should never let the personal information they've acquired about students adversely affect the teaching and learning process in their classrooms. A student's experiences, obstacles, and personal trials and tribulations should never serve as an excuse to lower academic standards or place limitations on what they think a student should be able to achieve. It is part of the teacher's job to help students push beyond their perceived limitations and circumstances. Teachers should always try to encourage and motivate students to go further than what they thought possible.

Finally, public schoolteachers are often asked to wear many different hats when interacting with students, but they should never let the extended duties and additional roles sidetrack them from their primary function: teaching. Teachers are not paid to be social workers, therapists, counselors, administrators, or psychologists. They should have empathy and a measure of compassion for students, but they're not responsible for solving every social, emotional, or environmental problems students face. Teachers are paid to deliver quality instruction; that is their primary function. Therefore, the end goal in gaining intimate knowledge about students is to ultimately use the information to help students achieve academically.

If public schoolteachers are able to help students achieve academic growth from one year to the next, then they have performed their role. You can't ask for anything more. Although all the extra duties that teachers perform for students are important on many levels, teachers can't allow the extra "stuff" to sidetrack them from their original and most important purpose, which is advancing students academically.

Assisting Students Academically

The entire purpose for teachers to develop a thorough understanding of their students is to assist them academically. While it is true that some teachers are able to teach students without knowing much about them, many of those same teachers will undoubtedly experience difficulties if or when their students start to show some form of resistance to the learning process. The resistance could stem from academic or behavioral deficiencies. During such times, intimate knowledge about students will become useful to teachers. It will inform teachers' decision making, and give them insight into the academic needs and deficiencies of the students having the most difficulties.

Teachers can often ascertain students' academic deficiencies from assessments and classroom observations, but that's not always the case. Sometimes, students reject assessments by not taking them seriously. Some students even suffer from test anxiety, or they behave in ways that bring negative consequences and attention. When this happens, teachers aren't always able to truly judge what students actually know.

When teachers work to establish trust and rapport, students are more likely to take academic risks. This is demonstrated when students raise their hands in an attempt to answer questions verbally, or in written form, even though they could possibly have the wrong answers. They will also be willing to ask for help when they don't know or completely understand something. This will give teachers opportunities to find out their students' strengths and weaknesses, apply methods and strategies to resolve students' academic deficiencies, reteach certain standards and objectives that students didn't completely master, or introduce new material to expand students' understanding and skill levels. This is how teachers can strategically address students academically, and help them achieve substantial growth from one calendar school year to the next.

Understand: Having thorough knowledge about students doesn't mean a teacher has to make accommodations for each individual student's needs with every lesson. That would not be feasible. In fact, not all students need accommodations, modifications, or have deficiencies that require special attention. The knowledge teachers acquire about students will be most beneficial when the teacher is trying to target specific needs and deficiencies. It will give teachers insight in the methods and strategies to use to create the optimal classroom learning experience for students collectively, and for those being targeted for additional support.

Remember: Before any academic concerns can be addressed, teachers need to develop a thorough understanding of the students sitting in their classrooms. Such information is acquired in different ways and over various periods, but the information will be beneficial to teachers when students show some form of resistance or when they need to create a plan to resolve students' unique academic deficiencies.

The rules students use on the playground are similar to the rules they subconsciously use in classrooms: Students do not play well or work with others whom they don't like, and they don't keep playing a game in which they always lose. In other words, students will be engaged as long as they think someone cares and is there to help, and as long as they believe there is a chance for them to be successful (White, Crouse, Bafile, & Barnes, 2009).

SUMMARY POINTS

- Teachers must be able to engage their students to effectively teach them.
- To engage students, teachers must have a deep understanding about them.
- All teachers should know three types of information about their students: global, local, and individual.
- Having intimate knowledge of students also helps teachers ease their anxieties and fears.
- Global information pertains to information on all students across the entire school district.
- Local information pertains to information specific to the school and community where the teacher works.

- Individual information pertains to the individual students on a teacher's classroom roster.
- Teachers should engage in relationship-building activities before academic activities.

3

RULE 2

Be a Facilitator

Public schoolteachers are charged with the duty of providing students with a high-quality education. To accomplish this task effectively, they should adopt a facilitation approach for delivering instruction. This means the learning activities and materials must be geared toward how students learn, and less toward how teachers like to teach. A facilitator teacher is not concerned with prescribed regimental forms of instructional delivery, but rather with providing students with learning experiences that help them grow and develop. They help students take ownership of their own learning by putting more emphasis on student-centered learning activities that will allow students to demonstrate what they've learned.

ORIENTATION[1]

After finding out that Caesar had taken Cleopatra's side, Ptolemy and his advisers plotted to kill them both. Ptolemy's general, Achillas, gathered all of the Egyptian soldiers and surrounded the royal palace, trapping Caesar and Cleopatra inside. Believing that Caesar was powerless, many citizens from Alexandria joined Achillas in the attack. Cleopatra's

---

1. The text in this section is a paraphrased narrative derived from facts presented by Roller (2010), Tyldesley (2008), Flamarion (1993), and Sapet (2007).

younger sister, Arsinoe, even got in on the act. She managed to join the soldiers and declare herself queen of Egypt and coruler with her brother. It was the beginning of a short-lived Alexandria war.

This war didn't particularly worry Caesar because he had been in similar situations previously, facing much tougher armies than Ptolemy's, but it was a little difficult for him to fight with only a small force at his disposal. Ptolemy first dammed the canals, which threatened to cut off Caesar's water supply. Then Ptolemy interrupted Caesar's communications by sea. But before Ptolemy and Arsinoe could totally move in, the rest of Caesar's army arrived from Syria and successfully put down the insurrection.

Both of Ptolemy's chief advisers were executed. Arsinoe was captured and taken back to Rome where she was paraded in the streets as a royal prisoner of war before being imprisoned. Ptolemy was later found drowned in the Nile River, still wearing his golden armor. Apparently, the weight of the armor was too heavy for him to swim while trying to escape the pursuing Roman soldiers.

With the death of her brother, Ptolemy XIII, and the imprisonment of her sister, Arsinoe, Cleopatra became the sole ruler of Egypt. Caesar had restored her position, but to maintain it according to Egyptian law, she had to marry her last surviving brother, Ptolemy XIV, who was only eleven years old at the time. He mysteriously died of poisoning less than four years after marrying Cleopatra. It is perhaps not a coincidence that Cleopatra became pregnant soon after this, and was not shy in naming Caesar as the father. Caesar never denied or acknowledged this claim. There was probably a part of him that wanted the child to carry on his name and dynasty, because his marriage to his wife Calpurnia did not produce a child. Cleopatra was surely aware that this gave her a hold on Caesar.

INTERPRETATION

When Cleopatra was a child, she witnessed a ruthless battle for power between her two older sisters, Cleopatra VI and Berenice. Berenice, the younger sister, murdered her elder sister and then her own husband in an attempt to take sole control of Egypt while their father was fleeing for his life in Rome.

Berenice's actions didn't sit well with many of her subjects. They wondered how someone of royal blood—a woman in particular—could commit such a horrible act against her own family members. This created many enemies for Berenice. Many Egyptians refused to follow her, and a strong resistance started to form. They didn't want to serve a queen who could commit such cold acts of violence against her own people.

Cleopatra learned a valuable lesson from Berenice: She would never be seen committing horrible actions of any kind; instead, she would always let someone else do the dirty work for her. Having someone else to do the work would allow her to keep her hands clean, and remain the embodiment of civility.

Early in her career, she used Caesar to do her bidding. He fought off threats from her brother Ptolemy by executing his advisers and quieting the rebellion. Caesar's efforts also led to the accidental drowning of her bother and coruler, which gave her sole possession of the throne. She also used Caesar to capture and imprison her younger sister, Arsinoe, which took care of all her immediate enemies and threats to her power. Later, she would use Mark Antony in the same way to defy Octavian, and later to execute her sister Arsinoe.

In both situations, Cleopatra stayed in the background, setting the expectations and tone for others who would actually perform the tasks she needed accomplished. She was the puppet master pulling the strings to make the puppets perform. She allowed others to do the work for her while she benefited from the aftermath.

KEYS TO TEACHING

In the traditional teaching model, teachers rely heavily on lecturing, bookwork, preprinted worksheets, and guided practice as the primary method of delivering instruction to students. Also associated with the traditional model are typical teacher behaviors: They do the majority of the talking during class time and mostly stand at the front of the room or sit behind their desks while students are expected to remain quiet in their seats and listen exclusively to the teacher. There is very little or no student-to-student communication, whole-class dialogue, or movement from students of any kind. If there is any unsolicited talking from students in any form, they are usually punished in some manner. The assumption in the traditional model is that teachers have and maintain all the knowledge while the students should be passive partakers in the learning process.

The traditional model of teaching is arguably the most practiced form of instructional delivery for most educators for two main reasons: First, most public schoolteachers are most comfortable when using this form of instructional delivery because it was the manner in which they were taught when they were in school. They were lectured for most of their educational experiences, so they are merely repeating what was done to them.

Second, there are some fear and control factors associated with using the traditional form. The fear is generally associated with what teachers think others might perceive as ineffective instruction. Many public schoolteachers dread having someone—an administrator, colleague, or parent, for example—walk past or into their classrooms and hear any resemblance of noise from students, or see anything that could be considered disorganized or dysfunctional classroom practices. Therefore, they deliberately go out of their way to structure their classroom activities to have students completely silent, immobile, and with paper and pencil in front of them.

This fear feeds teachers' insatiable desire to be in control of every aspect of the classroom. Teachers who fit this category think they must micromanage every aspect of the teaching and learning process—including all gestures, words, and actions from students. They believe that allowing students to converse, interact with each other, and move within the classroom during instructional time will lead to chaos and diminish their authority, so their classroom activities for students are often rigid, stale, and restrictive. Over time, teachers in this category resort to finding ways to keep students "busy" during class time, instead of creating ways to keep them actively engaged and learning. The combination of fear and control issues keeps public schoolteachers holding onto the traditional methods of delivering instruction.

The truth is that while some students might be able to learn from teachers who predominately use the traditional method of teaching, the majority of students within the average public school classroom today will lose interest and become disengaged; therefore, the quality of instruction being rendered to the majority of students over the course of a calendar school year will be minimal. The sad part is that many teachers who rely heavily on the traditional form of teaching truly believe they are doing a wonderful job. Some will even become highly offended if an administrator or anyone else tries to tell them otherwise. Teachers who teach predominantly from the traditional model are often under the illusion that they are teaching effectively because they are trapped on the "treadmill."

"Treadmill teaching" is based on the same premise as an exercise treadmill. When a person is running on a treadmill, his or her body is physically moving, but because the treadmill itself is stationary, the runner isn't really traveling any distance. No matter how hard or fast the person runs, he or she will remain in the same spot because the treadmill itself is not moving. The treadmill creates a simulated experience for the runner, which feels real and visceral because the runner might become tired, start sweating, and even burn several calories. The simulated experience makes the runner feel like he or she has run a great distance without having moved one inch.

Public schoolteachers who rely too heavily on the traditional form of instructional delivery also experience a treadmill effect. They are caught in a simulated experience of teaching, similar to that of the treadmill runner. They are not making the type of progress they think. At the end of the day, they too might be tired, frustrated, or experiencing other emotions associated with their daily responsibilities, duties, and interactions with various individuals (e.g., students, colleagues, administrators, and parents, to name a few). They feel like they are working hard, so they assume they are having the same effect on their students.

Because traditional teachers do the majority of the talking and moving during class time, they feel like they are doing a lot when they really are not. Their actions and movements within the classroom do not necessarily translate into high comprehension on behalf of the majority of their students. This simulated teaching experience is intensified as the school year progresses and they become further immersed in other duties and requirements such as writing lesson plans, adjusting to classroom issues, performing playground or other extended duties, attending conferences and meetings, dealing with student misbehaviors, setting and enforcing rules and expectations, interacting with colleagues, and connecting with parents.

When teachers are immersed in such tasks, they feel like they are teaching effectively because they are doing a lot of "stuff." The assumption is that if I'm this tired (or dealing with this much "stuff"), then I must be working hard; and if I'm working hard, then my students must be working hard as well and learning a great deal. The only problem is that the "stuff" these teachers are doing doesn't necessarily translate into engaging all students in the learning process, nor does it lead to students' mastering the content. When teachers are in treadmill teaching mode, they are unable to recognize the ineffectiveness of their instructional delivery. They are blinded by the visceral effects of the "stuff" they are doing each day to get by. If these teachers were able to step off of their "treadmill" and observe themselves, they would be able to see that the majority of the students in their classrooms are idle, bored, or passively engaged in the lesson—if there is any engagement at all.

When students are passive participants in the learning process, their energy level and enthusiasm for learning gradually diminishes over the course of the school year. The teacher might think students are paying attention, but they really are not. The teacher continues to talk, point, or write on the board while students give an occasional nod, smile, or show some other gesture to give the illusion of being engaged. Passively involved students will not raise their hands to answer questions or attempt to ask the teacher any questions, nor will they try to contribute anything meaningful. They will just keep nodding and gesturing until the class period is over, or they will totally check out and create behavioral problems for the teacher to manage, which will open up a separate bag of problems.

There may be a small group of students truly paying attention, but the majority will be merely pretending. It would probably be more beneficial for such teachers if all of their students were disengaged during the lesson, because then they might notice the ineffectiveness of their delivery. The one to three students who are answering questions and participating are unknowingly keeping their teachers in treadmill mode, and further disconnecting them from true engagement with the entire class.

Such teachers fail to notice that their questions, dialogue, comments, and feedback are directed only toward the few students who are actually responding to them. If this continues to happen over the course of a school year, the teacher will be unconsciously teaching only to a few select students. Eventually, the students who are not engaged will start doing one or more of the following: They will go to sleep in class, find something to distract them and totally tune the teacher out, become a behavior problem, or they might skip class and stop coming altogether. Teachers who work predominantly from the traditional model will produce low outcomes for the majority of their students over the course of the school year, and ultimately burn themselves out faster because the traditional method of teaching is not only ineffective at engaging all students, but it can also be exhausting because the teacher is doing all of the talking and movement for most of the school year while students merely sit and listen.

Furthermore, the traditional method of teaching also puts a heavy emphasis on multiple-choice, pen-and-paper assessments. These types of assessments are not inherently bad; they can be beneficial to the learning process if used appropriately, but they don't always serve as the best indicator to determine whether students have truly mastered the content. To keep students engaged, assess whether students have mastered the material, and to completely avoid burnout, public school-teachers should be like Cleopatra and adopt a facilitator approach to their instructional delivery.

A facilitator teacher is one who helps students discover knowledge on their own by mediating discussions, guiding meetings, proctoring study sessions, and using students' inquiry to lead the learning process (Levy, 2008). This approach is a mindset that teachers must adopt; they must get rid of disproportionate feelings of fear and control and replace them with appropriate thoughts of freedom and exploration.

The facilitator model of instructional delivery is more student centered and less teacher driven: It places emphasis on the tasks and activities that students have to perform to demonstrate to the teacher that they have mastered the content. This doesn't mean that facilitator teachers refrain from using lecture, guided practice, or worksheets as part of their instructional delivery and learning activities; nor does it mean that there are not times when facilitator teachers require students to be quiet and seated. The greatest difference with teachers who adopt the facilitator model over the traditional one is that they don't use the aforementioned instructional methods (e.g., lecturing, guided practice, worksheets, and restricting students) as their sole method of instructional delivery.

Also, the facilitator teachers' actions are different. They don't spend the majority of their time in front of the classroom standing at a chalk board or hunched over an overhead projector; instead, they are moving among their students, monitoring their progress as they work to complete the academic tasks and activities given to them. The facilitator puts the responsibility on students to become involved in their own learning. The facilitator's role is to introduce subjects of discussion, provide the necessary background knowledge, encourage sharing of perspectives, and integrate students' shared experiences.

A good facilitator is a connector and integrator, the glue that brings the collective experiences of the classroom together for shared learning (Levy, 2008). Teachers who use this model understand that it is not their role to dictate exactly how students should learn. Their role is more connected to guiding, inspiring, and encouraging students to learn. Being a facilitator is not something inherent to all teachers. It is a mentality they must work to develop, and a skill they must work at to craft. The following are some ways teachers can transition from the traditional form of delivery to the facilitator model:

- Allow students opportunities to dialogue and interact with each other, preferably during the completion of academic activities in class.
- Ask students multiple questions throughout the lesson.
- All lessons should be centered on students being able to demonstrate what they know or performing a certain skill successfully. There should be an emphasis on students being able to explore, create, dialogue, critique, and discover meaning.
- Communicate all directions and expectations clearly before releasing students to complete tasks and activities on their own.
- Make the content accessible and developmentally appropriate; use differentiation when necessary.
- Don't be afraid to let go of some control over the classroom. The teacher doesn't have to be the center of attention all the time or be the sole source of knowledge within the classroom. Trust that students will perform appropriately after you've modeled or explained what is acceptable.

Two popular structures best support the facilitator model of instructional delivery: Socratic seminars and reciprocal teaching. Each can be used by any teacher regardless of their content or grade level. According to Mangrum (2010) the Socratic Method, named after the classical Greek philosopher Socrates, is a form of inquiry and discussion. Teachers ask students a series of questions to stimulate dialogue, foster critical thinking, and to generate creative ideas. This method of questioning often involves a discussion or debate of one point of view versus another. By evolving students in a learning environment that's rich with communication and inquiry, students will be better able to learn and retain the concepts taught to them.

Likewise, reciprocal teaching also uses dialogue between teachers and students, except the dialogue is generated from a passage from some form of text. According to Pilonieta and Medina (2009), reciprocal teaching is a reading technique used to promote the teaching and learning process. A reciprocal approach provides students with four specific reading strategies that are actively and consciously used to support comprehension: questioning, clarifying, summarizing, and predicting. Reciprocal teaching is best represented as a dialogue between teachers and students in which participants take turns assuming the role of teacher (Pilonieta & Medina, 2009). It is most effective in the context of small-group collaborative investigation, which is maintained by the teacher.

Both structures are more student-centered instead of being more teacher-driven. Because the emphasis is placed more on the students, teachers will have more time to answer students' questions, respond to students' misunderstandings, and assist students toward mastery of the learning objectives—this is what the facilitator model is all about. This approach to instructional delivery allows teachers to provide the framework for learning (i.e., the lessons, objectives, expectations, and activities) while students are able to explore, create, grapple, dialogue, collaborate, discover, and arrive at correct meanings and answers on their own, without the teacher giving them all the answers or doing all the work. This also fosters higher-order thinking skills in students because they have to make connections, produce, create, and articulate what they have learned.

The facilitator model helps teachers immediately identify whether students understand the learning objectives and expectations because they are able to see it in the *work* students do. When students demonstrate to teachers what they know, teachers are able to get an accurate assessment of what students have or haven't learned. This information can be used by teachers to determine whether they should reteach or move on to the next unit, objectives, or set of skills. Also, with the facilitator approach, there is an appropriate balance between how much teachers talk during class time and what students actually do to demonstrate what they have mastered (Levy, 2008). In this case, the majority of the talking and activity within the classroom will come from the students and not the teacher.

The facilitator approach saves teachers valuable time and energy: It will prevent premature feelings of burnout and decrease their overall levels of stress. Understand: The majority of the *work* involved in the teaching and learning process should be done by students. More emphasis should be placed on what students need to do to prove to their teachers that they have mastered the content. All lessons and activities within the classroom should be designed so students are actively engaged in completing tasks. This approach will help students take more ownership over their learning, and decrease the chance of students becoming bored and disengaged.

SUMMARY POINTS

- Many teachers rely on the traditional method of delivering instruction out of fear and a need for control over every aspect of the classroom.
- The facilitator approach is more student centered and less teacher driven.
- Students become bored when they have to sit quietly and listen to the teacher talk for long periods, which leads to behavior problems and low achievement.
- Students need to be completely engaged in the classroom learning activities for true learning to take place.
- When a teacher acts as a facilitator, he or she assist students better by providing guidance as they work to discover knowledge or complete a given task or activity.

4

RULE 3

Create Interesting Lessons

Students respond best when they are presented with interesting content. Therefore, teachers should present students with lessons and activities that appeal to them. Teachers should not only engage students in a complete learning experience that causes all of their senses to tingle, but they should also get them to recognize the purpose behind what they are learning. Lessons should be like artworks, being creative as well as entertaining and appealing to students in many different forms. In doing so, learning will become fun and exciting to students, and it will feel less like a chore. It will also increase the chances that students will retain the information taught to them.

ORIENTATION[1]

In 47 BC, things were looking very promising for Cleopatra. She sat at the helm of the Egyptian empire; had just given birth to her first child, a boy whom she named Caesarion; and was allied with the most powerful man of the known world at that time—Julius Caesar, whom she named as her child's father. That same year, Caesar invited Cleopatra

---

1. The text in this section is a paraphrased narrative derived from facts presented by Roller (2010), Tyldesley (2008), Flamarion (1993), Pateman (1994), Miller and Browning (2008), and Nardo (2001).

and Caesarion to Rome. Even though Caesar never publically acknowledged Caesarion as his son, inviting him and Cleopatra to Rome as his
private guests gave both of them instant credibility.

Cleopatra obliged Caesar's request, hoping that the trip would bring
her closer to Caesar, extend her ties within the Roman Empire, and
legitimize her son. Her dream was to someday have her son succeed his
father and rule a unified Roman-Egyptian nation. Unfortunately for
Cleopatra, she would never see that day. Little did she know that things
were about to change for her, Caesarion, and Caesar.

During her stay in Rome, several members of the Roman Senate
assassinated Caesar. His murder sparked a civil war in which Mark
Antony, Octavian (Caesar's nineteen-year-old great-nephew), and others fought the Roman Senate for both revenge and power. Fearing for
her life, Cleopatra fled Rome and returned to Alexandria.

According to Caesar's will, Octavian was declared his successor and
adopted son, and in April of 44 BC he claimed his inheritance. Octavian's claim to the throne didn't sit well in all quarters. Antony was
particularly opposed to it, and so, most especially, was Cleopatra, who
considered it a slap in the face. After all, Octavian wasn't Caesar's bio-
logical son, whereas Caesarion was. There wasn't a word mentioned
about Caesarion in Julius Caesar's will.

The result of Caesar's death was anarchy and civil war in Rome.
When the dust settled, the empire was divided among three men: Octavian, Marcus Lepidus, and Mark Antony. Lepidus soon faded from the
picture because of his lack of political power. This left Octavian and
Antony. They divided Rome in half and each set out to rule their respective areas peacefully. Octavian controlled the eastern territories
while Antony controlled the western provinces. The peace didn't last
long because both men wanted more power: They each wanted to control all of Rome alone.

During the years Rome's political picture was sorting itself out and
taking form under Octavian and Antony, Cleopatra was extremely vulnerable in Egypt. She still needed a protector, and she still needed
Rome. She couldn't go to Octavian because he was recognized as Caesar's adopted son; her son Caesarion threatened his existence. Antony
was the best choice as an ally for several reasons. First, he was not only
the controller of the eastern territories of Rome, but he was perceived
to be the more dominant between the two: He was older and more

popular, the kind of man Cleopatra needed. But unlike Octavian, Antony was in great debt.

Antony was a great soldier and military leader. He was also ambitious; war seemed to bring the best out of him. As a civilian, Antony didn't possess the same qualities. He was known for his heavy drinking, partying with women, and insatiable desire for physical pleasures. The generosity he showed his soldiers combined with his own vices contributed to his dire financial situation. Antony, when stationed in the Cilician city of Tarsus, was busy raising funds throughout Gaul, Greece, Asia, and Cilicia to pay some of his debts. He demanded all that owed Rome to pay their debts within two years. Egypt was also in debt to Rome dating back to Ptolemy VII. Antony summoned Cleopatra to Tarsus in hopes of collecting on the debt Egypt owed to Rome.

Cleopatra knew that Egypt wasn't in any position to repay debts owed to Rome, but if she didn't pay, she risked losing Rome's support in the future. Considering all of her options, Cleopatra decided to put on a show that would rival anything seen during that time—something that would be talked about for ages. First, she ignored all of his initial letters summoning her to report to Tarsus. It wasn't until Antony sent his personal messenger that she decided to make the journey. Cleopatra sailed down the river Cydnus in a barge with purple silk sails and a gilded stern. The oars, made of silver, beat time to music provided by flutes, pipes, and harps. Incense perfumed the air while Cleopatra reclined beneath a gold-spangled canopy dressed in colorful robes similar to the deity Isis. She was fanned by small boys dressed as Cupids, and her maids were dressed like sea nymphs and graces.

The people of Tarsus flocked to the harbor to get a glimpse of the spectacle. The news of her arrival spread throughout all of Cilicia. Antony sent his messenger aboard Cleopatra's barge to invite her to be his guest for dinner at his quarters. She declined his invitation, insisting that he be her guest aboard her ship. Antony accepted and later dined with Cleopatra aboard her vessel. When Antony came on board, he was greeted by brilliant candelabras in all shapes and forms lowered from above. Cleopatra fed him from a banquet containing a variety of meats and delicacies, all served on plates of gold inlaid with precious stones.

During dinner, Cleopatra was dressed as the goddess Venus. Her body was scented lightly with rare perfume, and her dress revealed just enough of her body to make Antony wonder about the rest: Only her back, stomach, and arms were exposed, and, depending on the position in which she was standing or sitting, her leg would peek out of side slits of her dress. She also wore gold and silver jewelry on her ears, neck, and wrists. Cleopatra even had on an ankle bracelet that made a faint tinkling sound when she walked; her hair was also entangled with pearls. She was definitely a sight to behold.

Cleopatra was aware that Antony was beginning to associate himself with the deity Dionysos. She tried to create the atmosphere that their meeting was more that a meeting between two rulers, that it was rather a meeting between the "gods"—Antony got the point. The entire production, opulence, and grandeur overwhelmed and impressed Antony so much that he abandoned his original intention for summoning Cleopatra. He became so enthralled by Cleopatra that he decided to accompany her back to Alexandria where he spent the entire winter of 40–41 BC with her.

INTERPRETATION

It was obvious from the beginning that Cleopatra was trying to seduce Antony the moment she arrived in the city of Tarsus, but Antony didn't care, he wanted to go along for the ride to see where it would take him. This is what happens when a person's mind is totally stimulated and engaged: He or she becomes immersed in the experience, soaking in every aspect and detail.

Cleopatra knew that Antony wasn't from Rome's aristocracy, nor was he the intellectual type. He was a simple man who enjoyed pleasure: He liked to overindulge in food, women, and fun. Most of all, she understood that Antony, like most people, hated boredom and wanted to avoid it at all costs—in fact, this was the underlying cause of his drinking and debts. As a civilian, Antony yearned for excitement; he needed new adventures to explore and challenges to conquer. He turned to drinking and partying as a distraction to occupy his time.

The Antonies of the world always need something to do. They yearn for something, or someone, to entertain or distract them when their daily experiences become routine and banal. These types would literally go crazy if they found themselves with too much idle time on their hands. Boredom is their worst enemy because it usually leads them to destructive behaviors. Cleopatra knew that to win Antony over, she had to keep things interesting for him. When everyone else shunned Antony for his vices and bad habits, Cleopatra embraced him and his vices to ensure that the novelty never wore off. Their time together always had to be fresh and exciting, with never a dull moment. Cleopatra had to always keep Antony guessing, wondering, thinking, exploring, anticipating, hoping, and discovering.

To keep Antony engaged, she initiated a few simple moves. First, she made a deliberate effort to distinguish herself from the other leaders Antony had summoned to Tarsus. When the other leaders immediately came running after Antony's first invitation, Cleopatra ignored all of his initial requests and didn't appear before him until after he sent his personal messenger. This got Antony's attention and made an impression in his mind because she did the unexpected. This move also heightened the anticipation of her arrival. He wondered, "Who is this so-called queen who thinks she can ignore my summons and keep me waiting?"

Second, Cleopatra created a compelling spectacle, appealing to all of Antony's senses. She had music and tinkling objects for his ears to hear, beautiful colors and sparkling objects for his eyes to see, perfumes and incense for his nose to smell, food and pastries for his mouth to taste, and to touch. . . . Well, I'm sure you can figure that part out. They eventually got married and had three children together.

Everything Cleopatra did—the barge, costumes, servants, jewels, food, and her style of dress—was done with grandeur and splendor to keep Antony engaged and interested in her. Behind every door hid a new surprise for him; Antony didn't know what to expect from one moment to the next while in Cleopatra's presence. She charmed him from every angle, keeping him entrenched and enchanted in the atmosphere she created. She wanted him to believe that while with her, he was not in the presence of a mere mortal woman, but of a goddess. It's no wonder Antony was said to be defenseless against Cleopatra's charms.

KEYS TO TEACHING

Many public schools—especially those serving high concentrations of students from families living in poverty or of low socioeconomic status—are plagued by low achievement, poor student attendance, and a multitude of student-related disciplinary issues. Poverty, community environment, and lack of parental support are just some of the reasons often attributed to the problems many public schools experience.

While such issues are detrimental and have the ability to adversely affect students on many levels, the truth is that many of the problems associated with student attendance, academic achievement, and discipline can be either exacerbated or minimized, depending on the level of instruction delivered to students on a daily basis. Teachers can't control factors associated with students' economic status, home environment, or community dynamics, but they can control to a significant degree the activities that students experience within classrooms. Teachers can increase the level and quality of classroom instruction simply by increasing the level of student engagement.

According to White, Crouse, Bafile, and Barnes (2009), student engagement is increased when students are interested in the lessons and activities presented to them. Too many public schoolteachers do not understand the importance of engaging students with lessons that captivate and spark their interest. They teach in the same manner, using the same method for delivering instruction day after day whether the lessons appeal to their students or not. Their teaching methods do not take into account the different learning styles and modalities of the students in their respective classrooms. These kinds of teachers are more concerned with the way they feel comfortable teaching and delivering instruction, instead of adopting their style to the best ways students learn and retain knowledge.

Teachers who fit this category manufacture the same stale lessons year after year without any deviation, upgrades, or modifications. Within a short time, usually within the first few weeks of school, students become bored and disinterested. When students become bored, achievement will inevitably drop while issues such as absenteeism, tardiness, and disciplinary issues increase. This type of teaching is divisive and detrimental to the effectiveness of both students and teachers. When such problems in the classroom start to manifest, the ineffective teachers often mistakenly attribute the decline to the students' overall lack of desire for learning or their disregard for authority and classroom rules; in reality, that assessment is often far from the truth in most cases.

It is not uncommon for students to become turned off when encountering difficult or new subject matter; likewise, students will show various forms of resistance when presented with different topics. While this can be expected, the resistance that most students display toward learning (e.g., behavioral problems, absenteeism, low output, minimal effort, etc.) has more to do with students' inability to connect with the subject matter being taught. The disconnection is generally caused by the way in which lessons are presented instructionally by classroom teachers as opposed to the problem being solely with the students or the subject matter itself.

When teachers provide students with lessons that are interesting and delivered in a creative way, much of students' resistance to learning will be drastically reduced or completely eliminated, depending on the severity of the students' academic deficiencies and the teacher's level of creativity when designing lessons. Understand: Engaging students with interesting lessons is the cornerstone of quality teaching and learning. Teachers have to constantly look for ways to make their lessons creative and innovative. Most public school students are similar to Marc Antony in that they hate boredom. While engaged in any activity—whether at school or otherwise—they want their involvement to be something interesting and meaningful.

Just as Cleopatra did for Marc Antony, teachers have to create compelling spectacles in their classrooms to capture and maintain their students' attention. There can never be a dull moment during the lesson. This doesn't mean that teachers should have a fun activity for students every minute of a class period. There will be moments when students should sit still and listen. But it does mean that students should be engaged in something meaningful every minute they are in class.

Boredom and idleness are the enemies of effective student engagement, and death knells for the teaching and learning process. Studies have shown that boredom actually impairs one's ability to learn. When students become bored in the classroom, they usually look for something to fill the void, which is usually counterproductive to the learning process.

Although there is no one way to create an interesting lesson to engage students, the following is a general framework. This framework can be useful to all teachers because it can be modified and adapted to fit any teacher's particular grade level, subject area, and students. It will also help ensure that every student in the classroom has a positive and engaging learning experience.

Plan All the Way to the End

The first step in creating an interesting lesson is preparation. Teachers must take time to plan every detail of the lesson from start to finish, making sure every minute of class time is accounted for. There should not be any downtime, gaps, or idle moments within the lesson when students are engaged in a meaningful learning task or activity. Teachers shouldn't overplan or cram the lesson with meaningless tasks and busy work for students to complete because that would be counterproductive. The lesson must be constructed so students are actively participating and involved in meaningful activities that are appropriately organized. The learning activities should be sequenced so they are not only aligned to standards and objectives, but so they also provide students with a robust learning experience.

Understand: Effective planning is one of the most essential elements for creating interesting lessons. A lesson that is not well planned will be obvious to anyone observing, especially to students. Public schoolteachers must plan every detail of the lesson—considering everything from deciding which objectives and standards to cover, sequencing of the unit themes, determining the amount of time that should be spent on each learning activity, anticipating possible reactions and questions from students, identifying potential disruptions or interruptions in the lesson, deciding which equipment or materials to use, considering the various learning levels of students, selecting assessment tools for measuring whether students are grasping the concepts, and determining possible adaptations or modifications in the lesson based on students' needs just to name a few.

During the planning phase, teachers should ask themselves the following questions: What do I want students to learn? What is the best way to deliver this information to students? What activities will enhance the students' learning experience when covering this subject? How can

I deliver this in a way that will keep students interested for the duration of the class? Once I have students' attention, how will I keep it? How can I make the subject relevant to students? What are the materials needed to support this lesson? What questions can be asked to get students to really think? Which students are my high, middle, and low performers? How will I gauge whether students are learning? The answers to such questions will help teachers create lessons that are not only interesting, but also aligned to students' needs.

According to Ritchhart and Church (2011), the best way to engage students is to connect the lesson's activities to students' interests or the real world. Too often, students become disengaged because they don't clearly understand—or see the relevance of—how their work in the classroom connects with anything they experience outside of the classroom in their everyday lives. The average student will not attempt to learn something new if they don't see the value or importance of it. Merely telling students they need to learn a particular thing to get good grades or to pass the state's proficiency test is often not enough. Connecting the lesson's activities and tasks to things that interest students is the best way to keep and maintain their attention.

Engaging students with interesting lessons takes knowledge of students' interests, good planning, and time management. The key to encompassing all three is to break each lesson down into three distinctive sections. Every lesson should have a complete beginning, middle, and ending. Each section has its own distinct characteristics that will make up the overall effectiveness of the lesson. Also, the teacher's role and behavior will vary during each section of the lesson. All three sections combine to create a fruitful learning experience for students.

Starting the Lesson the Right Way

The way in which a teacher starts a lesson often determines the students' level of engagement. The beginning of a lesson can also significantly affect the learning activities that will be used for students to gain mastery of the subject matter, as well as the outcomes that students produce. Therefore, it is vital that teachers start their lessons on a strong note by leading with an activity that will grab students' attention. For a lesson to have a strong beginning section, it must have three distinct components—opening routines, a warm-up activity, and a formal introduction.

The opening routines help to settle students down as they enter the classroom. During this time, the students and teacher may go through a set of daily norms that govern how students should enter the classroom, including accessing materials, taking attendance, or collecting homework and other assignments, just to name a few. Depending on the age of the students and the time frame within the school year, the teacher's actions during the opening routines may vary.

For example, early in the school year a teacher will typically be more involved, vocal, and hands-on during the opening routines—directing students on what to do and where to go. But after a few weeks, when students have become familiar with the consistency of the opening routines, then the teacher can relinquish some of the control because students will be able to perform the tasks at the beginning of the class automatically without the teacher's assistance or prompting. After the routines are completed and the students have settled, then the teacher can transition students to the warm-up activity.

The warm-up activity—also referred to as the "Do-Now"—could be a question, writing prompt, scenario, short reading passage, or a problem for students to solve. The purpose of the warm-up activity is to get students focused, spark their curiosity, and to get them in a learning frame of mind. According to Johnson (2011) the "Do-Now" activity is one of the most important and effective strategies for engaging students and eliminating time wasted while trying to get students settled. Johnson identifies some common traits of all good warm-up activities:

- They are interesting, fun, and challenging.
- They are educational, not just time-fillers.
- They can be completed by all students within five to fifteen minutes.
- They can be accomplished independently, without the teacher's assistance.
- They are not always graded assignments, but do contribute to students' grades or mastery of the objectives.
- They are collected and filed, or discussed as a class or in small groups.
- They change periodically to add interest and avoid boredom.

It is important that teachers use their imagination and creativity when forming warm-up activities for students. Because warm-up activities are meant to introduce students to the lesson, it is best to have an activity that will grab their attention and spark their interest. If teachers do not capture students' attention within the first five minutes, it's going to be very difficult to maintain their interest and keep them on task for the remainder of the class period.

For example, when I was in middle school, I had a math teacher who was very good at creating interesting warm-up activities. Because he took the time to find out what we were interested in, he used that information and incorporated it into his warm-up activities. I remember one time he started the class period by holding up a life-size poster of the rapper LL Cool J. Back then, LL Cool J was the most popular rapper to all the students our age. His songs were being played on the radio, and many of the kids in our school revered him.

"Do any of you know the name of the person on this poster?" our teacher asked. We all responded enthusiastically, "Yeah, that's LL."

"Well, LL Cool J has a problem." The teacher went on to say, "His stage managers built a stage for him to perform during his next concert. The stage is 100 feet in length and 20 feet in width. They're trying to figure out how much security rope is needed to circle the entire stage. Your job for the next ten minutes is to help them figure out the answer to this problem. You can get with a partner or you can work alone, but you only have ten minutes to get it done."

In another scenario, the same teacher held up a poster of Michael Jordan, asking, "Do any of you know the name of the man on this poster I'm holding? I want you to pretend that you are Michael Jordan's personal trainer, and he wants you to calculate his free-throw percentage after one of his practice sessions. While shooting free-throws, he shot a total of 200. He made 179 shots and missed 29. What percentage of the shots did Michael Jordan make? What percentage of his free-throw shots did he miss? Write the number of free-throws made in a fraction. Is his free-throw percentage good or bad? Explain your answer."

In contrast, I had an art teacher in middle school who never started her lessons in the right manner. She didn't have any opening routines or tasks for students to complete upon entering her classroom, nor did she attempt to engage us with any meaningful warm-up activities before going into the meat of her lessons. The result was utter confusion and chaos. The students entered the art room as they pleased—talking loudly, running, and performing a host of other inappropriate behaviors that made it difficult for the teacher to start the lesson on a strong, positive note. Also, because it took a while for the class to settle, the effect of her lessons were greatly diminished. The off-task behavior students brought into the classroom carried over when the teacher began to teach, which adversely affected the teaching and learning process.

These examples are mentioned to show how important opening routines and warm-up activities are for capturing students' attention during the initial phase of a lesson. It is also important to note that teachers should follow up with students immediately after the warm-up activity is finished. The work from the warm-up can be discussed in small groups or as a class. Students should be allowed to share and dialogue about the work generated from the warm-up activity. This will give students immediate feedback, and reinforce the skills and concepts being taught. It is also the beginning of their investment in the learning process.

The last section of the beginning phase of a good lesson is the formal introduction. This is when teachers introduce the topic, unit, skills, standards, objectives, or subject matter that students will be working on that day. After the teacher has brought the warm-up activity to a close, he or she can proceed by reviewing the learning objectives and expectations with students. Such objectives should be posted for all students to see.

More importantly, this is the part of the lesson when teachers should perform learning-enhancement tasks like introducing and defining key vocabulary, providing background knowledge on the topic, scaffolding upon students' prior knowledge, and modeling specific tasks and skills. The formal introduction is where a little guided practice or lecturing can be useful. This is important because it is the precursor to the middle section of the lesson.

The beginning of a lesson—opening routines, warm-up activity, and formal introduction—should not exceed a combined twenty minutes. If this section of the lesson lasts longer than twenty minutes, it could only mean one thing: The teacher spent too much time on one of the components within the beginning section. Holding the beginning section to twenty minutes will help the teacher stay organized, and ensure that the lesson is well balanced.

The Middle or Body Section of the Lesson

After the warm-up activity is complete, teachers should transition students to the next phase of the lesson, which is the middle section. This is the part where the bulk of the learning activities will take place—leading students toward mastery of the curriculum, intended skills, objectives, or standards. It is also the section where teachers should spend the majority of their time. Depending on the length of the class period, teachers should prepare to have students engaged in at least two (no more than three) different learning activities that are all aligned to the lesson's objectives for any given lesson.

This is important for several reasons: First, it adds rigor to the lesson. A rigorous lesson is one that is complex in nature, and it takes some effort on the part of students to master (Jackson, 2011). When a lesson has rigor, students are not able to breeze through it quickly; they must think their way through the process, or complete a series of steps to reach the intended goals. Rigor requires students to construct meaning for themselves, impose structure on information, integrate individual skills into the process, and apply what they have learned in more than one context (Jackson, 2011). Lessons that have two to three learning activities create layers for students to work through. Such lessons are multidimensional, foster critical thinking, and challenge students to grapple with concepts in different ways.

Second, having more than one meaningful learning activity will reduce the number of student disciplinary issues within the classroom. I've heard many teachers and school administrators say the best remedy for student behavioral problems in the classroom is a good lesson. I would go a little further and say the best remedy for student behavioral problems in the classroom is an *interesting* lesson. When lessons are interesting, students will have neither the time nor desire to misbehave because they will be completely invested in the learning process and focused on the tasks placed before them. Understand: When academic deficiencies are not an issue, most students misbehave only when they are disconnected from the learning process. A rigorous lesson based on students' interest will provide students with the stimuli that will keep their creative energy following, which will foster appropriate behaviors from students.

Last, multiple learning activities (focused on the same standard or learning objective) will prevent a lesson from becoming monotonous and boring—especially if the activities connect to different learning styles. This allows students to change the way they work, think, and interact within the classroom while trying to master the material. They have to perform different tasks and operations and use various skills—which builds on their knowledge and enhances their cognitive understanding and learning experiences in the classroom. As their cognitive levels increase, they will begin to ask questions, pursue knowledge, and take more ownership over their learning.

Giving students a maximum of two different activities on a particular standard or learning objective will also help teachers gain a clear picture of the types of lessons students respond to most favorably and the reasons why. Favorable activities can be repeated at various times throughout the school year with different units, standards, and objectives. This will help maximize students' output and foster the best results.

When creating activities for students during the middle section of the lesson, teachers should incorporate tenets from the five major learning styles—auditory, visual, tactile, kinesthetic, and interpersonal and social (Pritchard, 2008). Components from these modalities will assist teachers with varying their classroom learning activities, which will also help to keep students interested.

The idea of individualized learning styles originated in the 1970s from the work of Neil Fleming (Pritchard, 2008). Fleming defines his theory as "an individual's natural or habitual pattern of acquiring and processing information in learning situations" (Pritchard, 2008). Each learning style describes the best ways that people like to learn and retain knowledge. Fleming created the VAK model, which focused on three main sensory receivers: Visual, auditory, and kinesthetic receivers were used to determine one's dominant learning style. The model was later expanded to include tactile and interpersonal/social learning styles. Proponents for the use of learning styles in education say teachers should assess the learning styles of their students and adapt their classroom lessons and activities to fit those natural dispositions toward learning.

For example, auditory learners learn best through hearing (Pritchard, 2008). They respond best to activities such as discussions, tapes, lecturing, and reading out loud. Visual learners learn best through visual stimuli (Pritchard, 2008). Students who have a preference for this style think in pictures like visual aids, overhead slides, diagrams, colorful imagery, and handouts.

Tactile learners learn best when they are able to work with their hands and manipulate objects (Pritchard, 2008). They favor lessons that are based in active exploration, experiments, and the use of their hands. Kinesthetic learners learn best through activities that require movement, such as participating in any physical activity, sports, or playing instruments (Pritchard, 2008). Lastly, social or interpersonal learners learn best while interacting with other people. Students who favor this learning style benefit from dialogue, discussions, and collaborative and group activities.

Understand: Just because a student (or students) has a predisposition for one particular learning style doesn't mean teachers should strictly adhere to that particular style as their primary form of delivery, nor does it mean that students are only able to learn from one particular method. It is a good practice for teachers to create various lessons that expose students to many different learning styles, modalities, and skill sets. In fact, this is how the human brain learns and retains information. Therefore, different experiences will expand one's brainpower and increase the student's ability to learn and retain knowledge. Depending on the lesson, subject matter, and grade level of the students, the lessons teachers create throughout the school year should expose students to elements of all five learning styles.

This means that one day the classroom activities might incorporate tactile and interpersonal learning styles; the next day, the lesson might involve visual and auditory styles—all while working within the same unit theme or set of objectives. Just because a student is a tactile learner doesn't mean he or she shouldn't have opportunities to experience interpersonal ways of learning. The goal is to mix things up. Diverse classroom activities will help students develop different skills, and strengthen areas where they may need improvement the most.

It is also important to note that the middle section of the lesson is also the time when teachers can act as classroom facilitators, and not be the sole drivers of the entire instructional process. As facilitators, they can move around the room, monitor students actions, check for students' understandings and misunderstandings, answer students' clarifying questions, and keep students on task.

Likewise, teachers can have students work in small or large groups or individually, or teachers can differentiate instruction based on the learning levels and cognitive abilities of the students within the classroom. The middle section of the lesson should be viewed by teachers as the time when students apply what they've learned in ways that are tangible and meaningful. This reinforces mastery of learning, helps students retain information, and creates an even balance between teacher-driven instruction and student-centered learning.

Students should be actively involved and participating in every lesson. With active participation one can clearly observe students responding to teacher-generated questions, observe dialogue and movement, and students raising their hands and generating their own questions just to name a few. During the middle section of the lesson, students should be doing the work while teachers observe, monitor, evaluate, and provide support and clarity.

Finally, the middle section of the lesson is also where teachers can assess whether students have learned the concepts or mastered the skills taught to them. Unless a formal assessment is given to students like a test, quiz, or exam, teachers should have informal assessments built into the learning activities. Informal assessments could include but are not limited to asking probing questions, monitoring students' work, having students verbally explain what they are working on, and having students demonstrate their knowledge in some form. These, and other types of informal assessments, allow teachers to get an accurate pulse of what students have and have not learned. This will dictate whether to move on to the next unit or set of objectives, or to reteach the same objectives until students have mastered a particular skill.

Bringing the Lesson to a Close

The last section of a lesson is called the *ending* or *concluding section.* Some teachers like to refer to this section as the "exit ticket." It should take place during the last ten to twenty minutes of the class period. This is the time when teachers should bring closure to the lesson by briefly recapping what students were supposed to have learned for the day, or having students perform some objective-related task before leaving the classroom.

This is critical because it is the teacher's last chance to leave a lasting impression on students, and cement the skills and objectives they were trying to convey. They can also use this section of the lesson to give out homework assignments, answer last-minute clarifying questions, clear up any final misunderstandings, and have students participate in closing routines and procedures.

This is also the section of the lesson that ineffective teachers fail to execute. Usually because of poor planning and disorganization, many teachers squander this time in one or more of the following ways: First, they have no real objectives or skills for students to master, so they merely try to give students "busy work" until the class period ends. Second, by the time the class period is down to the last twenty minutes, students are disengaged to the point where they are falling asleep or exhibiting some other off-task behavior, which causes teachers to misuse their time by putting out one fire after another.

Another problem some teachers have associated with this area is that they often allow students to remain on one particular activity or task too long, so the class period expires before the teacher has a chance to bring the lesson to a complete close. Or because there wasn't any balance in the lesson's activities, students were only able to work on one set of skills, while the others were neglected.

Remember: The ending is just as important as the beginning of the lesson. It is the precursor to the lesson that will be taught the next school day. Ending a lesson on a bad note will increase the chances of starting the next lesson the same way. It is also important to remember that having a variety of activities when creating lessons is the key to maintaining student engagement and reducing boredom and off-task behaviors. Variety was the main element Cleopatra used to keep Marc Antony captivated—she keep him engaged in one pleasurable activity after another. Having variety in the lessons is also the necessary ingredient for teachers to keep students engaged, participating, and learning.

Presenting students with various learning activities will make students' learning experience qualitatively rich. They will be able to build on knowledge and skills they already possess, and see the interconnectedness between the old and the new skills acquired. Teachers who try to create the most interesting lessons will discover that over time, their students will begin to care less about the fun or excitement associated with a lesson, and care more about the act of learning itself. This is how teachers are able to instill a love for learning among their students.

Teachers who use only one method of delivering instruction do themselves and their students a great disservice. Doing so places limitations on their own teaching prowess, neglecting the development of skills that could enhance their own professional practices and effectiveness. Even more detrimental is that teachers who use only one method of instructional delivery are in danger of developing only one group of skills in their students, and they run the risk of only engaging a small group of students within their classrooms. Students who only know one way of learning will find it hard to conceive the potential that exists within their own minds.

SUMMARY POINTS

- Preparation is the cornerstone of effective instructional delivery.
- Every lesson should be structured so that it has a beginning, middle, and end.
- The beginning section of a lesson consists of opening routines, warm-up activity, and formal introduction.
- The beginning section of a lesson should not exceed twenty minutes.
- The middle section of the lesson is where the bulk of the learning activities take place.
- Learning activities should incorporate tenets from the five major learning styles.
- Teachers should vary the learning activities with each lesson.
- The ending section of the lesson is used by teachers to bring closure to the lesson.
- The ending section of a lesson should be done during the last twenty minutes of the class period.
- A good lesson reduces the number of student misbehaviors.

5

RULE 4

Manage the Classroom and the Students Will Follow

Classroom management will always be a critical area of concern for public schoolteachers. It encompasses more than dealing with student behavioral issues; it also deals with how well a teacher organizes the learning activities, maintains order and safety, establishes daily routines and practices, and implements classroom procedures while delivering quality instruction. It also encompasses the actions teachers take to create an environment that supports and facilitates both academic and social-emotional development. Teachers who are able to manage their classrooms successfully will be able to deliver a quality educational experience to their students.

ORIENTATION[1]

Cleopatra and Marc Antony spent the entire winter of 41–40 BC together. They spent most of their time in "play and diversion," squandering and fooling away time in enjoyments. They called themselves and the band of friends who partied with them the "Illimitable Livers," and

---

1. The text in this section is a paraphrased narrative derived from facts presented by Roller (2010), Tyldesley (2008), Flamarion (1993), Pateman (1994), Miller and Browning (2008), and Nardo (2001).

they lavished entertainments on one another with an extravagance beyond what was known in Rome.

Antony's baser habits—his heavy drinking, gambling, bawdy behavior, and womanizing—began to dominate his personality. Aside from participating in weekly orgies, he led Cleopatra and other friends down the back streets of Alexandria disguised as a rowdy gang of commoners. They knocked on people's doors and ran away before the owners of the homes answered.

Cleopatra participated in such escapades to keep Antony interested and to ensure that he remained loyal to her. One Roman historian, Plutarch, wrote the following about their relationship:

> Plato admits four sorts of flattery, but Cleopatra had a thousand. Since Antony was seriously disposed to mirth, she had at every moment some new delight or charm to meet his wishes; at every turn she was upon him, never letting him escape her neither by day or night: she played at dice, drank, and even hunted with him. Cleopatra was also with him when he exercised in arms. At night she would go rambling with him to disturb and torment people at their doors and windows, dressed like servants.

Still, even among the endless partying, Cleopatra never forgot her true purpose and never missed an opportunity of reminding Antony what that was. If any proof was needed that Cleopatra had established a firm hold on Antony, it was his obedience to her order to have her sister Arsinoe killed in the temple of Artemus Leucophryne at Miletus, where Caesar had placed her. Cleopatra never forgave Arsinoe for her betrayal during the siege of the palace at Alexandria. As long as Arsinoe was alive, she would always be a threat to Cleopatra's rule in Egypt. One day, Cleopatra lied to Antony by telling him that Arsinoe was planning an attempt on his life because of his affiliation with her. Sensing that Arsinoe's demise would please Cleopatra, he immediately moved to have her murdered behind the temple walls.

In the spring of 40 BC Antony left Cleopatra and returned to Rome after learning that his wife, Fulvia, and his brother, Lucius, had declared war against Octavian. He didn't want to leave Cleopatra, but he needed to go back to Rome to try to undo what his wife and brother started. Antony did not see Cleopatra again for four years. Six months after Antony returned to his duties in Rome, Cleopatra gave birth to twins, Cleopatra Selene and Alexander Helios.

During the four years that Antony was away from Egypt, his Roman wife Fulvia died. He soon married Octavian's sister Octavia. Antony agreed to the union for two reasons: First, Octavian would be less likely to ally against Antony if Antony were married to Octavian's sister; second, the Roman public, which intensely disliked Cleopatra, would be pleased by the marriage and more amenable to his rule.

During all this time, Antony never forgot the pleasures of Egypt and how much he wanted them. In 37 BC, he again visited Cleopatra. While set for an invasion of Rome's enemy, Parthia, Antony met Cleopatra in Antioch, Syria, and there, on the Orontes River, the two were married. The fact that Antony was already married made no difference to him. The union was not honored in Rome, but it was accepted in the eastern part of the empire and in Egypt. In addition, it legitimized the twins born to Cleopatra. Later, Antony and Cleopatra's third child was born, a son named Ptolemy Philadelphus.

Antony was so enthralled by Cleopatra that he didn't devote his full attention to the battle against Parthia, and was badly defeated. Even after his defeat, Cleopatra provided Antony with food, clothing, and money for his army. Then, in a move that annoyed Rome, Antony presented Cleopatra with territories that were essential to Egypt; these lands included Cyprus, the Cilician Coast, Phoenicia, Syria, Judea, and Arabia. Egypt could now build ships from the lumber from Cilician Coast—and Cleopatra proceeded to create a vast fleet.

In a desperate attempt to boost his ego after his defeat with the Parthians, Antony turned his attention to the minor kingdom of Armenia, whose king he captured in 34 BC. Antony could have followed the custom of taking a vanquished ruler to Rome, where the defeated leader was displayed before its citizens. This action would likely have restored some of Antony's lost prestige. Instead, Antony ignored the custom and brought the Armenian king to Cleopatra's feet in Alexandria. This act infuriated Rome, and to make matters worse, Antony formally recognized Cleopatra's oldest son, Caesarion, now thirteen years old, as the true son of Julius Caesar—a declaration which also angered Octavian. From then on, Alexandria became Antony's home. He never went back to Rome again.

INTERPRETATION

There are many Roman historians who believed that Cleopatra placed some magical spell over Marc Antony. How else could she have been able to control his behavior? The truth is that she didn't use magic to control Antony's actions, but instead strategically controlled Antony's environment, which dictated his behavior. She always had something new for him to try, some place for him to go, or some activity for him to do. Cleopatra led him from one pleasurable experience to the next—enthralling him in every event. She never allowed him to become bored or complacent.

Cleopatra was able to accomplish this by fulfilling Antony's wildest fantasies. While he was in her presence, she made him forget about his obligations and responsibilities to Rome, which were often complicated and burdensome. This made him feel special and more alive. To him, she was like an oasis in a dessert. Antony enjoyed being around Cleopatra; therefore, he willfully did whatever she asked of him. Her careful manipulation of Antony's environment made him neglect his original agenda in the best interest of Rome in exchange for following the agenda Cleopatra set for him in the best interest of Egypt.

In addition to controlling Antony's environment, Cleopatra also periodically changed her behavior patterns. She was flattering, complimentary, accommodating, and attentive to his every whim for 90 percent of the time she and Antony were together, often putting on grand spectacles to dazzle him. In contrast, whenever she wanted him to do something for her, or when she noticed his attention was slipping, she withdrew from him completely or became introverted. Antony would notice the changes in Cleopatra's behavior, and then he would inquire to find out the reason for the changes.

This is the point when Cleopatra would reveal what she wanted him to do. Since he desperately wanted Cleopatra to return to her normal behavior, Antony was willing to do anything in his power to make her happy again—even if it meant abandoning his Roman wife and family, honoring Egypt with conquered cities, or murdering Cleopatra's older sister. Leading Antony's day-to-day activities eventually led to him committing acts on Cleopatra's behalf.

Cleopatra knew that if she asked Antony directly to perform a certain task—such as murder her sister Arsinoe—he might refuse or put up some resistance. Instead, she chose a more subtle approach. Cleopatra understood that by controlling Antony's environment (e.g., the places he went, the food he ate, the people he saw, and the things he did) she could indirectly control his behavior without him being aware she was doing so. She made him believe that he was forming opinions and making decisions of his own accord, even though all of the decisions he made mostly benefited Cleopatra.

KEYS TO TEACHING

Classroom management is, and always will be, one of the most talked about topics for teachers—especially for those working in public schools that have a history of failure. With the advent of federal legislation such as the No Child Left Behind Act, increased emphasis on high-stakes testing, and the standards-based education movement, a public schoolteacher's ability to effectively manage the classroom has become more vital than ever before.

Typically, when teacher effectiveness is evaluated, classroom management is one of the first things considered. Teachers are often judged on their ability to establish and maintain order within the classroom so it can function appropriately. With classroom management being such an important issue, it's ironic that most university teacher education programs spend very little time on this subject.

Most aspiring teachers receive the bulk of their teacher training around educational theory, ethics, lesson planning, curriculum development and implementation, and assessments. A very small percentage of their training is devoted to classroom management because the university student is expected to learn classroom management in the field during their few weeks of student-teaching, or gain such knowledge once they actually receive a paid teaching position.

This becomes problematic for new teachers because they leave their respective universities with a degree in education, but they lack proper knowledge to effectively perform a critical aspect of the job. They have a keen understanding of their content areas, but most of them lack proper understanding of how to effectively handle student discipline and the adverse behaviors students present that can get in the way of the learning process.

I am not advocating that areas of study such as ethics, curriculum, assessment, lesson planning, and other topics are not important; but many teacher university programs do not realize that classroom management is more about psychology than pedagogy. No matter how well teachers know their content areas, if they do not have a general understanding about how to deal with adverse student behaviors, then their ability to manage their classrooms will be minimal, and it will adversely affect their overall success as a teaching professional. Understanding the human side of teaching—the attitudes, behaviors, moods, frustrations, actions, and temperaments of students—is just as important, if not more important, as anything else.

Another reason many teachers have poor classroom management is because they approach it using the wrong framework. They make the mistake of trying to directly control the students' behavior by restricting their ability to move, dialogue, and interact with each other in the classroom. Such efforts also stifle students' creativity, foster various forms of resistance, and hinder their overall educational development.

Effective classroom management is not something that teachers do to students, but rather something they should experience with students. Instead of trying to devise ways to directly control students' behaviors, teachers should spend time controlling the classroom environment. If the classroom environment provides students with a rich learning experience that's organized, thoughtfully structured, and orderly, the students will respond accordingly.

The following is a framework that teachers can use to create an environment conducive to learning, which will improve their ability to manage their classrooms effectively and foster greater participation from students. The following strategies will improve any teacher's classroom management skills providing that the tenets discussed in the previous chapters have been incorporated into the teacher's normal practice. Those strategies are not only the foundation for effective teaching and student engagement, but are also the building blocks for effective classroom management.

The following classroom management strategies will inform teachers' decision making and help them make better connections with even the most difficult students. If Cleopatra was able to get Antony to abandon Rome, award her with conquered cities, and commit murder by controlling his environment, then surely a public schoolteacher can get students to comply with basic classroom rules, behave appropriately, and become engaged in the learning process.

Make the Classroom Conducive for Learning

Environment plays a huge part in how one behaves. Therefore, the first thing teachers must do is create an atmosphere conducive to learning. According to McDonald and Hershman (2010), the environment teachers create for students is equally as important as the content taught and the learning strategies used. An atmosphere conducive to learning can be created by taking some time to properly decorate the classroom, arrange seats, position furniture and equipment, and establish learning spaces and centers to name a few.

The classroom should be a visually stimulating place. When students walk into the classroom, they should instantly know it is a place of learning based on what they see around them. The following are some suggestions teachers can use to make their classrooms more stimulating:

- Plants
- Unit themes
- Bulletin boards
- Word walls
- Maps and charts
- Posted student work
- Motivational quotes and sayings
- Content wall posting and hangings
- Pictures of prominent historical figures
- Posters of celebrities who positively endorse education

This is not an exhaustive list. Teachers should be as creative as possible when decorating their rooms. They should add their own personal touch, while being mindful not to go overboard. It is not necessary to plaster every square inch of the walls. The goal is to stimulate and beautify, not to crowd and clutter. The room décor will help get students in the right mind frame the moment they enter the classroom, which will set the tone for everything else students experience during the learning process.

Strategically Arrange Furniture and Equipment

After teachers have decorated their classrooms, their next focus should be on the arrangement of the classroom furniture and equipment. This is a vital area that is instrumental for creating the right classroom atmosphere. Furniture and equipment are usually bulky and tend to take up a lot of space. These items are also the most expensive and will be damaged or broken if they are not arranged properly by teachers or used appropriately by students. Therefore, teachers must strategically arrange furniture and equipment so these items do not detract from the learning environment. Items that typically take up the most space in a classroom include things like the students' and teacher's desks, bookshelves, file cabinets, electronic equipment (computers, projectors, recorders, etc.), and storage closets.

With the exception of the electronic equipment and the students' desks, such items should be placed along the walls or in corners. They can even be decorated to camouflage their appearance. All items that do not serve a useful purpose should be removed from the classroom. Removing items that are not beneficial to the learning environment will instantly make the classroom look roomier and enhance the room décor. Electronic equipment such as computers and other related items should have a designated area near electrical outlets. All other equipment should be stored and locked away until the teacher is ready to use it.

The following are some questions teachers should consider when arranging classroom furniture and equipment:

- How will students access classroom supplies?
- How should the students' desks be arranged?
- Where will students put unfinished and gradable work?
- Where will I put textbooks and supplemental materials?
- How many students can this classroom hold comfortably?
- How will students be able to move and interact in the classroom?
- What learning centers and work stations will I have? In what part of the room should I place them?

Classrooms should be arranged in a way that teachers, students, and visitors can move throughout the room freely without bumping into things or each other. The designated areas in the room (work stations, computers, activity centers, supply areas, etc.) should be labeled for students. If applicable, there should also be instructions posted that indicate how students should use such equipment and work areas. The expectations for using equipment and work areas should be reviewed by the teacher, and referenced often until students demonstrate the desired level of understanding or behavior. This will establish consistency and reinforce classroom norms.

The most important furniture item in the classroom is the students' desks. Many teachers, especially novice ones, do not take enough time to arrange the students' desks properly, which can lead to increased classroom management problems. Many teachers simply put the desks in rows or create a seating chart from a pregenerated class roaster. Putting desks in rows makes it easy for custodians to do their jobs but doing so is not necessarily beneficial for effective classroom management. The desks should be moved and arranged to accommodate the type of instruction being delivered to students, and so that teachers can see every student in the classroom.

Develop Classroom Rituals

Once the room is transformed into a stimulating environment conducive to learning, the next step is to develop classroom rituals, which are also referred to as *classroom traditions, norms,* or *practices.* Classroom rituals occur in the classroom frequently: Students are able to experience these things on a daily, weekly, or even monthly basis. Rituals are important elements of effective classroom management that teachers must vehemently work to establish and maintain. They not only add to the fluidity of the class, but they also give students a sense of security, consistency, stability, and comfort because they know what to expect.

Some of the most common classroom rituals among all teachers are created to facilitate the following areas:

- Late arrivals
- The start of class
- Taking attendance
- Working in groups
- Dismissal from class
- Starting assignments

- The use of equipment
- Social behavioral norms
- Working in stations or groups
- Entering and exiting the room
- Signals to get students' attention
- Emergency drills and procedures
- Procedures for finishing assignments early
- Students moving around the room
- Make-up work and grading policies
- Collection and distribution of papers
- Classroom awards and recognition
- Collection and distribution of materials
- Going to the restroom and other places
- Procedures for dismissing the class

When I was a classroom teacher, one of my daily rituals was to post the lesson's objectives, agenda, and a warm-up "question of the day" on the board for students to see. Students knew where to look to find the agenda, to grab their books and relevant materials, and to start working on the daily warm-up question immediately upon entering the classroom. This simple ritual helped me to start my class off in a well-organized manner.

It is important to note that the rituals teachers establish must be explained clearly to students and practiced until all students completely understand. Teachers should not assume students will automatically know what to do, or properly interpret the expectations on their own. The bulk of the time spent with students during the first few days of school should be devoted to establishing, reviewing, and practicing classroom rituals, and they should be revisited periodically throughout the school year as needed.

Teachers should also establish rituals that are fun, which will have students looking forward to the experience (McDonald & Hershman, 2010). I know of an elementary school teacher who designated a new student every week to be the line leader as part of her classroom ritual. In fact, she assigned various positions and tasks to students, and she periodically changed the students performing such tasks.

Remember: Classroom rituals are important because they create a sense of familiarity for students, which allows them to feel more comfortable and receptive to learning. As students become familiar with the classroom rituals, they will be able to perform them automatically with very little prompting from the teacher, which enhances the teaching and learning process.

Classroom Rules and Consequences

Every game, sport, activity, or institution has rules for success, and consequences for participants who do not comply. A well-functioning classroom is no different. It requires participants to follow rules to be successful. Teachers need rules in place so their classrooms can operate smoothly, and so students understand the expectations that govern their behavior. Classroom rules are an essential part of effective classroom management, and necessary for creating a classroom conducive to learning (Kaiser & Rasminsky, 2007).

Before forming classroom rules, teachers should ask themselves the following questions:

- What is my preferred teaching style? How can I adapt it to meet the learning styles of students?
- What rules need to be in place to ensure the teaching and learning process is carried out successfully each day?
- What do I need from students to ensure that I am able to deliver instruction effectively? How will my classroom rules coincide with the classroom activities associated with the daily lessons?
- What are the things that I absolutely will not tolerate in class (the nonnegotiable items)? What are the issues on which I might be more flexible?
- If a student violates one or more of the classroom rules, how will I respond? How will I respond if a student verbally disrespects me?
- What are appropriate consequences that I can consistently administer in the classroom without involving the school's administration?
- What strategies or procedures can I use to maintain order and safety for all students in the classroom?
- How will I deal with major behavior problems?
- What are misbehaviors that necessitate a referral to an administrator?

- When should I attempt to contact parents? Which problems should I try to address solely with the student?

A necessary step in establishing standards of acceptable behavior in a classroom is to set rules of conduct (Partin, 2009). According to Kaiser and Rasminsky (2007) teachers should establish three to six rules to govern their classrooms. It should not be an exhaustive list beginning with "thou shall not," but a short list of rules that teachers think are important for the overall well-being of the classroom and everyone within it. The rules should be written clearly so all students can understand them, and they should be posted in the classroom to serve as a daily visual reminder.

The most powerful approach to forming classroom rules is to get the students' input and their assistance when developing them. Giving students a say in the rules that will affect them is the most strategic way for teachers to gain students' acceptance of the rules. Having students assist in the formation and implementation of the classroom rules lets them know that their opinions are valued. This will further strengthen the rapport between them and their teachers.

Similar to classroom rules, the consequences for breaking a rule should also be clearly understood by all students, free of ambiguous language, and posted in the classroom. Student collaboration and input should be encouraged for this as well. Consequences should be progressive by design, leading to different stages of discipline. The teacher should attempt to handle student disciplinary issues in varying degrees before sending the student out of class to an administrator. The following is just one example of possible progressive consequences:

- First offense: Verbal warning
- Second offense: Parental contact or student-centered action
- Third offense: Detention or alternate student-centered action
- Fourth offense: Student and/or parent conference
- Fifth offense: Written behavioral contract or student-centered action
- Sixth offense: Referral to the administrator
- Restart the process after the administrative referral

This example is designed to give teachers a bit of flexibility when trying to hold students accountable, and it also gives them a few options when trying to deal with adverse student behaviors. Teachers should not "empty the bank" too soon. This means they should move progressively through levels of consequences, making sure students are aware of every step. Also, when enforcing the rules and consequences, the teacher must exercise fairness and consistency.

Understanding Resistance from Students

Just because a classroom has a set of rules and consequences doesn't mean the teacher is going to get total compliance. Designing the rules and reviewing the expectations with students is the easy part, but gaining 100 percent compliance is where the real work must be done. Despite all the work teachers might do to establish rapport with students, they still should expect to receive some level of resistance from students at different points in the school year for various reasons. Resistance from students is not a problem in itself; the problem comes from teachers who don't know how to deal with it.

Teachers should not view resistance from students as an affront to their teaching abilities or authority, nor should they necessarily assume the student resisting is unteachable, unruly, or disrespectful. Understand: Resistance from students is one of the best indicators to let teachers know when they are gaining ground with their students. Sometimes, greater resistance from students means a greater chance to positively influence their behavior.

The resistance displayed by a student is nothing more than a manifestation of his or her deficiencies or an attempt to gain attention. The student might appear to be angry, unruly, defiant, and disrespectful, but the behavior is nothing more than an outward defense mechanism developed to avoid feeling hurt, embarrassed, and ashamed; or there could be a strong desire for the student to gain attention—whether positive or negative—to combat inner feelings of neglect. Teachers should view the resistance also as the student's official calling card for help. A student's adverse behaviors generally predates the present moment when the teacher is experiencing it in the classroom. The behaviors could stem from problems in the student's home environment, issues with previous adults and teachers, a deficiency in an academic skill that the student is trying to hide, or a lack of one or more basic needs (e.g., food, clothing, shelter, or emotional support).

Understand: When teachers are faced with adverse behaviors, or resistance from students of any kind, the important thing to remember is that the resistance is not exclusively directed at them. Instead of taking the student's adverse behavior personally, teachers should view it as a disguised call for help. Public schoolteachers must understand this to properly manage their classrooms, and provided the educational support students need and deserve.

I often compare student resistance to the resistance a fisherman experiences when trying to reel in a big fish. Once caught on the fishing rod, the fish will resist by tugging, pulling, and jerking. Some fish will even jump out of the water in an effort to free itself from the hook caught in its mouth. If the fisherman wants to catch the fish, he has to withstand the resistance by holding on to the rod, pulling back, and staying with it until the fish gives up.

The same is metaphorically true when dealing with a misbehaving student. When teachers experience resistance from a student, they should stand their ground and "dig their hooks deeper" to totally win the student over. The figurative hooks are the teacher's efforts to make connections, create a learning-conducive environment, build and establish rapport, reinforce classroom rules and consequences, and maintain contact with parents or some caring adult.

When faced with resistance, teachers should not back down. They should meet the resistance with an appropriate consequence, and then dig deeper to find out the underlying reason for the resistance. Then the teacher can create a strategy aligned with the student's unmet needs. Eventually, the misbehaving student will stop resisting if the teacher has applied all of the aforementioned tactics, just like the fish caught on the fisherman's line stops resisting.

It is also important to note that the teacher's actions play an important role in how students behave, and they often determine the level and frequency of the resistance they face. For example, teachers who act timid and unsure of themselves usually bring out the lion in students who wouldn't generally misbehave. A teacher who is a pushover will have an extremely difficult time gaining respect from students. On the other hand, teachers who act too authoritative, rigid, and uncompromising will prompt students to rebel out of anger. A teacher's actions and behavior must be within the habitable ground where they can be nurturing, yet corrective; understanding, yet stern; firm, yet fair; and instructional as well as managerial.

As mentioned earlier in this chapter, Cleopatra constantly changed her behavior toward Antony whenever she wanted him to behave in a certain way. She was flattering, complimentary, and attentive to his every need to gain and maintain his attention. But when she noticed his attention going in a direction counterproductive to her agenda, she changed her behavior by withdrawing all kindness and affection. This tactic can also work when dealing with students' behaviors.

Teachers must show students two sides of their behavior: One side is very helpful, understanding, and attentive to students' needs, and the other side is more corrective and unrelenting in the pursuit of maintaining order and a healthy classroom learning environment. If teachers have successfully implemented the aforementioned classroom rituals, rules and consequences, and room décor, students will undoubtedly select the helpful side because it will be to their benefit.

This will let students know that the teacher is serious about maintaining order within the classroom, and they'll think twice before behaving in an inappropriate manner. Remember: Teachers who are consistent, fair, and confident in their actions will not only gain respect from their students, but will also reduce the amount of resistance they could face throughout the course of a school year.

Dealing with Extreme Student Behaviors

The aforementioned strategies for fostering effective classroom management will work on 99 percent of students the average teacher will encounter on a yearly basis. The strategies will not work on the remaining 1 percent because they are the students with the most extreme behavior patterns. They do not respond to all of the same stimuli as the majority. I refer to these students as the "Extreme Supremes." Following are a few indicators to let teachers know when they are dealing with an Extreme Supreme student:

- The student could possibly have multiple academic or social deficiencies.
- The student is very sensitive, emotional, or has a tendency to overreact to the most trivial situations.

- The student exhibits behaviors such as profanity toward students and staff, constant attention seeking, refusing to follow simple directions, arguing and fighting with peers, or defiance toward authority figures.
- The student has the power to captivate the other students' attention and influence their behavior.
- The student lacks boundaries for what is acceptable or unacceptable within the classroom.
- The student may have a side that is abnormally rude, calculating, and malicious.
- The student's parents are usually unresponsive or unable to deal with the student's behaviors.
- The student will repeat the same detrimental behaviors even after being corrected multiple times and after receiving several progressive consequences.
- The student never takes ownership of his or her behavior.
- The student may have been physically or emotional abused at some point in his or her life (Yisrael, 2012).

Usually when there is trouble within the classroom, it can be traced back to one individual—the one who seems to be set on causing continual disruptions. On the surface, it may seem like multiple students are misbehaving, causing trouble, and detracting from the learning environment, but if teachers analyze their disruptive classroom situations closely, they discover that their problems started with one student's extreme behavioral tendencies. If public schoolteachers are honest with themselves, the disruptions increased because of their own inability to effectively handle the chronically disruptive student.

Disruptions appear to come from multiple students because the other students are merely following the path that the extreme student has paved. Students carefully monitor every word and action of their classroom teachers. They want to see if their teachers' actions match their words. When the nonextreme students observe their teachers' inability or unwillingness to handle an extreme student, it signals that they will be able to get away with the same or similar behaviors. Before the teachers realize it, they will have multiple students displaying inappropriate behaviors in the classroom at the most inappropriate times.

Conversely, if teachers are able to effectively deal with the Extreme Supreme's behavior, they will not only gain the other students' compliance, but they will also gain their respect. The nonextreme students will believe that if the teacher is able to effectively deal with a student they know is a chronic behavior problem, then it will be easy to deal with students who present fewer challenges. Therefore, a teacher's ability to recognize and effectively deal with an Extreme Supreme is critical. It could literally set the tone for the entire class, and affect how much the teacher is able to teach students throughout the school year.

The following sections are a three-step framework teachers can use when dealing with students who exhibit the most extreme behaviors in the classroom. If implemented correctly, the strategies will neutralize any attempts by the extreme student to disrupt the classroom learning environment.

Step One: Strategic Action

The strategies described in this chapter will be enough to effectively handle most behavioral problems and resistance teachers will face from most students, but it takes some skill to deal with a student with extreme behavioral deficiencies. When the extreme misbehaving students go on the attack, they usually direct the majority of their aggression directly at the classroom teacher. This is usually done for three main reasons: First, the student wants to maintain a certain status among his or her peers within the classroom. By challenging the teacher, the Extreme Supreme earns respect and admiration from the other students in the class. The reaction received from peers is an element that fuels the Extreme Supreme to behave more outlandishly.

Second, the extreme student is trying to test the limits of the classroom teacher. Extreme Supremes want to see if they can push the teacher's buttons or make the teacher lose control or waiver on any of the rules or consequences. If the teacher shows any inconsistency, timidity, or lack of control, all is lost. The Extreme Supreme will keep pushing until the class is in total disarray. Eventually, other students within the class will also start misbehaving.

Lastly, directing aggression and disrespect at the teacher is one of the best ways for the student to hide his or her academic deficiencies. This type of student has learned that if he or she does something to get under the teacher's skin, there is a high possibility that he or she will be immediately thrown out of the classroom or left alone. If the student is out of the class, then no one will know about the issues he or she is hiding. In most cases, the student would rather be kicked out of class than have someone find out he or she cannot perform some basic academic task or activity. For teachers to reach students like this, they must be able to see past the fronts these students display.

Understand: There are going to be some exchanges between the teacher and the Extreme Supreme. The exchanges could occur at different points within the school year, but the sooner the better. The exchanges between the teacher and student will usually follow a certain sequence of events, but if each exchange is handled correctly, the teacher will be able to drastically reduce or totally eliminate the undesirable behaviors being displayed by the student.

The first thing teachers can expect to see is minor misbehaviors that will occur frequently. Teachers might notice similar actions from other students, but the Extreme Supreme will display minor misbehaviors at a higher rate than normal: He or she will consistently violate multiple classroom rules and exhaust the consequences rather quickly. The minor behaviors could include but are not limited to chronic tardiness, random loud outbursts in class, distracting others, excessive amounts of horseplay, constantly being off task, failure to follow simple directions, refusing to participate in learning activities, reckless and defiant behaviors, misuse of equipment, and refusing to answer questions when called on.

To combat these minor behaviors, the teacher must respond quickly to send the proper message that disruptions—no matter how minor—will not be tolerated. Some teachers make the mistake of ignoring the misbehaviors, hoping the student will stop on his or her own, but the student never does. The student will get progressively worse if the teacher doesn't act swiftly.

Swift action can come in many forms. Depending on the behavior, the teacher may decide to verbally reinforce the expectations, change the student's seating arrangement, pull the student aside for a brief conference, use a time-out, or contact the student's parents. It is important for teachers to maintain their composure during these initial exchanges. This will show the other students watching that the teacher is in control, and is serious about maintaining order and a positive learning environment.

After the teacher has successfully dealt with the minor behaviors from the Extreme Supreme, then he or she will start to take it up a notch. The teacher's swift action on the minor misbehaviors is going to cause discomfort and irritation with the Extreme Supreme because he or she wasn't able to accomplish the intended goal. Because the teacher didn't respond as the Extreme Supreme predicted (e.g., ignoring the student, losing control, putting the student out, etc.), then the student will try to go even further.

The next level from the Extreme Supreme could come in the form of verbal disrespect toward the teacher. This is the point where 90 percent of public schoolteachers throw in the towel and give up. As soon as they are verbally disrespected they either become fearful and do nothing about the student's behavior, or they try to do everything in their power to keep the student out of their classroom. Both are counterproductive responses.

In actuality, verbal disrespect is usually the Extreme Supreme's final attempt at disrupting the classroom or getting what they want. Over the years, these types of students have learned that if they show this side of their behavior, they will get the affirmation they were trying to achieve. When a student displays this form of misbehavior, the teacher should smile because the student has run out of ammunition—he or she doesn't have anything else left. Verbally disrespecting the teacher is their ace in the hole or trump card. They believe that if they use a little profanity or make some derogatory remark, then the teacher will either kick them out of class or bend to their influence. When verbal disrespect fails, they don't have anything else to use.

It is important to note that along with the verbal disrespect, teachers might observe such students exhibiting minor forms of intimidation (violation of space), inappropriate hand gestures (pointing and waving of hands), profane terminology and derogatory name calling, door slamming, misuse of furniture and equipment, and verbal threats. Again, teachers should not take such behavior from students personally. It is the Extreme Supreme's last attempt at a power move to disrupt the class, get his or her way, cover up academic deficiencies, and maintain the adoration of his or her peers (Yisrael, 2012).

For example, when I was a classroom teacher, an Extreme Supreme exploded on me because I didn't allow him to sleep in class. He put his head down on three separate occasions. The first two times I gave him verbal warnings. The third time I noticed he had fallen completely asleep. So I politely tapped his shoulder and suggested that he go into the hall to get a drink of water to help wake up. He responded by shouting, "Get your damn hands off me, and leave me alone!"

I responded by saying, "Listen, you will not speak to me in that manner again. I want the same respect that I give to you. Now you can either sit up and participate with your classmates, or you can use my phone to contact your mother to see how she feels about your behavior."

In my example, I tackled the undesirable behavior (head down, disrespect), reinforced the desirable behavior (sit up and participate, speak to the teacher appropriately), and followed up with a consequence among alternatives (participate with the class, call the student's mother). Depending on the severity of the behavior being displayed, the teacher may elect to not give an alternative consequence. Some behaviors are so severe that the student must be told exactly what to do, or be completely removed from the class to preserve the learning environment for the other students.

In the aforementioned scenario, the student continued to use more profanity toward me and would not comply with my request to start participating. I eventually had to call for the school's security to have him removed from my classroom. It was the only way that I was able to continue teaching. This is typical Extreme Supreme behavior. When given a consequence among alternatives, the Extreme Supreme will normally elect the choice that is most defiant or against the teacher's wishes. This is just part of the game that Extreme Supremes like to play. This is done because the student has an audience (his or her peers in class) so the student wants to keep up the image (whatever that may be). When this happens, removing the Extreme Supreme from his or her peers could be the best action to take.

Step Two: Applying Corrective Action

This brings us to the next stage: the corrective action process. This is the follow-up after extreme behavior has been displayed. When some teachers send a misbehaving student out of the classroom, they tend to think that they've gained some sort of victory simply because the student was temporarily removed from the classroom. In reality the teacher hasn't really accomplished anything. Yes, the student was sent out of class, or maybe even disciplined by the principal or some administrator, but when the student returns to class, the negative behavior will start all over again. This happens to most teachers because they fail to apply corrective action after the student has been sent out.

To even come close to correcting the student's extreme misbehaviors, the classroom teacher must be part of the disciplinary process after the student has been put out of the classroom. Because the situation started with the classroom teacher, it's only right that the situation end with the teacher as well. To provide corrective action, the teacher (and the administrator overseeing the discipline at the school) should isolate the student away from his or her peers—preferably in an office, conference room, or place where students do not frequently visit. This will take away the student's peer audience and remove the student's desire to show off or create a scene.

In isolation, the student will be more likely to listen to what the teacher and administrator have to say. The teacher should use this time to ask some of the following questions:

- What causes you to behave in this way?
- Is there something else you want to talk about?
- What can I do to help you adjust better in class?
- How could you have handled the situation differently?
- What should you do next time if you're ever in a similar situation?
- Did something happen before class, or at home, that you want to talk about?
- How would your parents feel if they knew how you were behaving in class?
- If you were in the teacher's shoes, how would you have handled a student who was behaving in the same manner as you?
- Why are you so angry, and how can I help you?

While discussing the situation with the student, the teacher's demeanor should be very calm. The teacher should use clear and concise language while speaking and look the student directly in the eyes. Even though the teacher is speaking about a very severe situation that happened in the classroom, the teacher's demeanor and attitude should never be aggressive toward the student. The goal is to change the behavior, not to get revenge. The teacher should view this meeting as a potential turning point with the student, and it should be handled with care.

During the follow-up meeting, the teacher should pay extra attention to the student's demeanor. Students in such a situation will usually feel uncomfortable. Without a crowd or peers watching, students will be like fish out of water. They will try to do anything that will end the meeting quickly. Typical behaviors displayed by a student in such a meeting are as follows: long pauses between answers to questions asked, staring at the floor, looking away from the person talking, stuttering and muttered sentences, refusing to answer questions, becoming reclusive, pretending not to understand, and displaying an emotional breakdown (usually crying).

Despite the student's attempt at getting out of the meeting, the teacher should never allow the student to dictate the pace of the meeting. The teacher should deliberately slow down, recap the situation, and get the student to verbalize the problem and take ownership of his or her actions. Once the student takes ownership of the problem, then he or she will be receptive to adhering to future expectations, rules, consequences, and classroom norms.

Understand: The extreme behavior patterns that a student displays in the classroom are normally not a part of the student's real character or personality, nor do they usually have anything to do with the classroom teacher. The student is either trying to hide some academic deficiency, or some issue associated with his or her home environment. The misbehaviors or bad attitude are only a false image the student has manufactured to avoid embarrassment or pain, or to gain some form of attention or acceptance.

Classroom teachers are often witnesses (or victims) of such misbehaviors because they are the ones who are paying the most attention to the student on a daily basis, or they are trying to hold the student accountable for some action or standard of behavior. Once the teacher gains knowledge of the student's issues, whether academic or otherwise, then the teacher and school officials can strategically work to resolve them. This will ultimately strengthen the bond between the student and teacher. The student will start to see the teacher as a supporter instead of a foe.

Step Three: Administering Consequences

Finally, the most critical piece in this process is for the student to receive a consequence for the behaviors displayed. This final element cannot be left out; it is part of the student's learning process. He or she must understand that for every action there is a reaction, and that there are consequences for behaviors that disrupt the learning environment. The student must also understand that he or she is not only disrupting their learning time, but also the learning time of other students as well.

Even though the student could be suspended for the behaviors displayed in class, that's probably not the right course of action to take during the initial follow-up meeting with the student. While the student is receptive to listening to what the teacher has to say, the teacher should confirm the students' understanding of the rules and expectations. The student should also be made aware of future consequences if similar behaviors are displayed. A good idea would be to give the student an alternative consequence instead of suspension after the first follow up meeting, unless the behavior displayed in class was too egregious.

A few final points before concluding this chapter: First, when dealing with student behavioral issues, the teacher must make a strong connection with the parents or some concerned adult. This connection must start early in the school year, and must be an ongoing process. Parental engagement is important to the corrective process of the extreme student's behavior. When and how teachers decide to inform parents during the corrective process is totally up to them, and the rapport they've established with the student's parents previously.

Second, there are some rare instances when a teacher will encounter a student whose academic deficiencies are just as extreme as the social-behavioral deficiencies. Such a student might be a candidate for special education services. Again, such a referral should only be made under the most rare and severe cases. As mentioned previously, the majority of students will comply based on the teacher's organization, routines, norms, fairness, consistency, and relentless passion for maintaining order. A much smaller group will comply after parents are contacted and consequences have been assigned.

The severe behavioral students, an even smaller group, will comply after a corrective follow-up meeting (assisted by the parents, counselor, or a school administrator). Students who take teachers through the aforementioned steps multiple times and do not show any signs of changing their behaviors will likely be the ones who will need special education services. In this case, special education services might be exactly what the student needs to be successful in school.

To be effective at classroom management, teachers have to take the same approach as a gardener who grows a plant. A gardener doesn't try to force the plant to grow. He or she merely provides the right conditions (soil, water, proper sunlight, fertilizer, etc.); the plant will do the rest on its own. The aforementioned strategies will help teachers create the right conditions that will foster effective classroom management, which will ultimately lead to quality teaching and learning. Focusing on the conditions that make an environment conducive to learning is the best way for teachers to curtail misbehaviors, keep the classroom organized, and foster effective student engagement.

SUMMARY POINTS

- Teachers should put more emphasis on controlling the classroom environment, and lesson attempts to control students' behavior. Control the environment and the students will follow.
- Rules and consequences are necessary to provide structure, organization, and order within the classroom.
- The rules and consequences should be established on the first day of school and reviewed, modeled, and revisited for at least the first two to four weeks and periodically throughout the school year. This will firmly cement the expectations, which will decrease the types, and amount, of issues the teacher will have in the future.
- Teachers should spend significant time decorating the room and properly arranging the classroom furniture.
- The classroom rituals occur frequently. They help to create a sense of normalcy and familiarity for students.

- It is a good practice for teachers to include their students in the development of classroom rules and consequences.
- Resistance from students is usually a disguised call for help.

6

RULE 5

Create and Maintain Good Relationships with Parents

Obtaining true parental engagement in some public schools can be as difficult as trying to hit the moon with a stick. Despite the difficulties and obstacles that some parents may present, it is of great importance for teachers to form solid relationships with them, and work to build long-lasting partnerships. A teacher's ability to create and maintain working relationships with parents is invaluable. Parents are the first teachers of their children, so it is unrealistic to think that long-lasting or permanent growth in students—whether academically or behaviorally—will take place without the parents' support. In many instances, parents can be a teacher's greatest ally.

ORIENTATION[1]

Cleopatra was starting to realize that her dream of a united Roman-Egyptian Empire was not going to happen, but she still had Egypt, and she meant to keep it by any means necessary. Octavian declared war on Antony and was coming to Alexandria to get him. Cleopatra's forces alone could not stop Octavian, so she decided to negotiate with him.

---

1. The text in this section is a paraphrased narrative derived from facts presented by Roller (2010), Tyldesley (2008), Flamarion (1993), Pateman (1994), Miller and Browning (2008), and Nardo (2001).

When Octavian arrived in Phoenicia in the summer of 30 BC, he was met by emissaries from the Egyptian queen. Cleopatra's message was clear: She would vacate the throne if her son Caesarion, now age sixteen, was crowned king of Egypt. As for Antony, he asked only that he be allowed to live out his life in Egypt.

Octavian ignored Antony entirely and answered only the message from Cleopatra. He responded by saying she could save herself and her kingdom if she gave up Antony or executed him. Cleopatra would do neither—but knowing that her son Caesarion's life was in danger, she immediately sent him away from Egypt.

In the early hours of August 1, 30 BC, Antony set out from the palace with his troops to face the Roman troops, but he was forced to watch in despair from a hilltop as his remaining fleet and cavalrymen surrendered without putting up much of a fight. Antony could do nothing but return to Cleopatra's palace in utter defeat.

Meanwhile, Cleopatra heard of the surrender and knew the end was near, so she barricaded herself in her memorial building. When Antony returned to the palace, he was told that the queen had committed suicide. Believing that Cleopatra was dead, Antony decided that he did not want to live either. In the Roman custom, he took out his sword, put it to his chest, and fell upon it. Marc Antony didn't die immediately, however. When palace servants found him, they hoisted him on ropes through a window of the room where Cleopatra was barricaded.

Upon seeing Antony near death, Cleopatra became hysterical. She threw herself on him, covering her garments in Antony's blood. Antony died at age fifty-one in the arms of Cleopatra.

After Antony's death, Cleopatra received another message from Octavian. He told her that if she surrendered, she would not be harmed. Cleopatra replied that she would leave her chamber only upon Octavian's word that her children would remain as rulers of Egypt. Octavian agreed, but Cleopatra didn't believe him. She suspected that Octavian would promise anything to get what he wanted. She believed that in addition to taking the riches of Egypt, he would parade her through the streets of Rome in chains—something she could not tolerate. She refused to surrender. On the day of Antony's death, Octavian's soldiers broke into the monument and captured Cleopatra.

Several days later, Octavian prepared to leave for Rome, taking Cleopatra and her children with him as prisoners. Cleopatra received word of his plans and panicked. She envisioned the spectacle she and her children would create for the Romans because they greatly despised her. If she could not fulfill her destiny to restore the glory of her ancestors, she was determined that she would at least die in a manner that honored their greatness—one of her own choosing. She wrote a letter to Octavian asking him to bury her body next to Antony's when she died. She bathed, dressed in her royal finery, and ate a festive meal. Then she allowed herself to be bitten by a poisonous snake that had been smuggled into her chamber in a basket of figs by one of her servants. When Octavian's servants found her, she was dead, lying on a bed of gold with her servants also dead at her feet (she commanded her servants to allow themselves to be bitten by the snake as well). She was as impressive in death as in life. The extraordinary Cleopatra VII, queen of Egypt, the last of the Ptolemies to rule, was dead at age thirty-nine.

INTERPRETATION

When Cleopatra first came into power, she always had a strong ally to help sustain her success. When she first had trouble with her brother, Ptolemy XIII, who was coruling Egypt with her at the time, she sought refuge in the land of Syria. This ally allowed her the space to reevaluate herself, build an army, and make plans for returning to Egypt.

Later, Cleopatra was able to develop strong ties with Rome's Julius Caesar and Marc Antony. These individuals were able to protect her from other enemies, assist her with difficult tasks and situations, advise her in matters of war, and help to advance her goal of protecting Egypt and retaining independence. Having allies is important because they not only provide protection and resources, but they also help to remove obstacles. The right allies can help clear the path and open doors that will allow one to be more successful at achieving set goals and endeavors. The moment Cleopatra did not have a strong ally on her side she became vulnerable.

For example, on the day that Caesar was murdered, Cleopatra had to flee Rome immediately for fear of an assassination attempt on her own life. Caesar's death also put the stability of Egypt in jeopardy. Without Caesar as a protector, all of Egypt's debtors—including Rome—would have been out for blood. After Caesar, Cleopatra bonded with Marc Antony. He was a good ally to have, but her own actions got in the way, so the partnership wasn't as successful as it could have been. She took too much of Antony's time away from his obligations in Rome. This caused him to lose touch with his support base, and it allowed Octavian to gain a decisive advantage over him.

In the absence of a strong ally, Cleopatra lost her throne, lover, children, and even her own life. No matter how great or charismatic Cleopatra was as a person and ruler, she could not do it without help: She needed a partner with mutual interest who was invested in her success. The lack of a strong ally greatly contributed to her downfall.

KEYS TO TEACHING

Cleopatra's demise serves as a metaphoric warning to public schoolteachers. No matter how dynamic you might be as a teaching professional, you still need a strong ally with shared mutual interest to help you achieve and sustain the highest levels of success within the classroom. The most important, and most valuable, partner that a teacher can have is none other than the parents of the students they teach. Parents have the most invested in the classroom teacher's success because it is their children's education at stake.

One of the most important tasks public schoolteachers must accomplish is to form and maintain solid relationships with the parents. The quality of such relationships will affect nearly every aspect of the students' classroom experience—especially in the areas of student behavior and classroom instruction. When such relationships have been firmly connected, parents can open avenues for teachers that they would not have otherwise imagined.

To establish a strong relationship with parents, public schoolteachers must be persistent and diligent in trying to make the parent-teacher relationship work. A few questions teachers should ask themselves when thinking about forming and building relationships with parents follow:

- What type of parents am I working with (highly engaged, participatory, or minimally involved)?
- What is the best way to communicate with parents?

- What type of information are my students' parents most interested in?
- How often should I attempt to make contact with parents and for what reasons?
- What are the parents' expectations?
- What kind of relationship do I want to have with parents?
- When is it necessary to contact parents about classroom issues? When is it not?
- In what ways will I attempt to keep parents informed about what's going on in my classroom?

This is not an exhaustive list. The questions are there merely to get teachers thinking about parental engagement, and how they will attempt to foster it. The answers for many of the aforementioned questions will greatly depend on the parents' overall relationship with the school, and the dynamics of the community where students and families live. These questions also serve as the foundation for how teachers should attempt to include parents in the teaching and learning process.

Many public schoolteachers miss the mark when it comes to engaging parents. Many teachers only think of parental engagement in the abstract without truly working to make it part of their everyday practice. They know parental engagement is important because it is one of the many constructs littering the public educational landscape, but many teachers haven't fully grasped a complete understanding of the concept.

Some teachers believe effective parental engagement on their part is merely informing parents about student behavioral issues. Other teachers believe that it is their job to only teach students; they view maintaining strong relationships with parents as a waste of their time if they have to put forth a significant amount effort. Two of the most popular notions about effective parental engagement is having parents volunteer in some capacity at the school (e.g., make copies, host bake sales, sponsor clubs, sell school paraphernalia, etc.) and having parents show up for conferences and special events.

This kind of thinking is as much false as it is disconnected from what true parental engagement is all about. Much of this kind of thinking from teachers about parental engagement is mostly fostered by school administrators. Typically, if the school's administration doesn't have parental engagement as a top priority, then most teachers will echo the same sentiments.

Many public schoolteachers often confuse parental engagement with parental involvement. Parental involvement is connected to issues that generally benefit the school or the classroom teacher like volunteering, conferences, and school events. Parental engagement can encompass such things, but there is much more to it. Parental engagement is based more on the parents' interest—their needs and desires as they relate to the school and their children's overall quality of education.

Many parents can be difficult, uncooperative, and sometimes unresponsive when it comes to trying to include them in the teaching and learning process. Some teachers encounter parents who try to interfere in every little detail of the classroom, while other teachers struggle to get parents to become involved in any activity or event—but this doesn't mean teachers should not continue to work at building such relationships.

All public schoolteachers can foster effective parental engagement by incorporating the following principles: (1) Know the parent population thoroughly, (2) communicate with parents early and often, (3) organize well-planned activities that involve parents, and (4) recognize parents whenever possible. These four principles will help public schoolteachers effectively engage parents, and help them develop more meaningful educational experiences for students.

Know the Parent Population Thoroughly

Developing an understanding of the parent population is similar to gaining an understanding of students: It involves gathering and analyzing data associated with the community and cultural dynamics where parents live. This will help public schoolteachers understand certain norms, values, and feelings that parents have related to the school and their children's educational experience. Some useful information includes but is not limited to unemployment rates, community statistics (housing, crime, income, etc.), religious affiliations, types of grassroots and community organizations, dynamics of the school's parent-teacher association, and the levies that have passed or failed within the last ten years.

This kind of information will be immensely powerful for teachers. The information can be used not only to make genuine connections with parents, but also to reach students cognitively and on a social-emotional level. The tenets mentioned in chapter 2 will assist teachers in gaining the necessary information they need to develop a complete understanding of their students' parents.

In addition to the aforementioned strategy, teachers should create opportunities where they can ask parents about their expectations for their children's educational experience. This can be done through questionnaires, surveys, or by verbal communication. It really doesn't matter as long as parents are able to express their expectations and teachers are open to receiving them. It would also create opportunities for teachers to share their expectations as well. This will set the foundation for open dialogue, mutual respect, and constant communication between the teacher and the parents—therefore shrinking the distance between students' homes and the classroom.

Communicate with Parents Early and Often

Teachers should start communicating with parents early in the school year. Before the first day of school, teachers should send a letter or e-mail to all parents to introduce themselves. This initial communication should be positive, stressing how excited they are to be working with them and their children. By the end of the first week, another letter or e-mail should go out. This second communication should come with a syllabus, or detailed description of how the class will be structured (e.g., aspects of the curriculum, grading and attendance procedures, classroom routines and norms, assessments, academic pacing guides, and school rules, just to name a few).

At the end of the second week, leading into the third, teachers should plan to make at least one phone call or some other form of contact (e.g., e-mail, postcard, text message, newsletter, etc.), to the parents of every student on their class rosters. By this time, teachers should be more familiar with their students. Some assignments have been given, and they have assessed students' behaviors and some academic skills. The main purpose of the contact in the third week is to help teachers build a constant presence, which will allow parents to become familiar with them. This will lead to rapport and trust building.

After the third week, teachers should make it a habit to make some form of positive contact with parents at least once per month during the first semester, in addition to all other forms of contact that might be less positive. The teacher can report something positive the student did in class or elsewhere in the school building. Once teachers have established rapport with any given parent, then the positive monthly communications can be reduced to a bimonthly basis or as needed.

This increased effort on the part of parents is necessary because many parents today are very mistrustful of teachers, and in some extreme cases, parents have taken an adversarial stance toward public schoolteachers. The reasons for this vary greatly among school districts, but many teachers only attempt to communicate with parents when there is bad news to report. Because of this, some parents often become defensive when teachers contact them. To them, contact from any school official usually means something is wrong or that the child is in trouble. The increased positive communications with parents will allow parents to relax, and help to break down their defense mechanisms.

The constant communications will make parents more receptive when having to listen to a negative behavioral report. Over time, the parents will grow to appreciate the teachers' efforts and view them more as partners in their child's educational experience, instead of adversaries.

Have Well-Organized Parental Activities

The fastest way to have parents question the integrity and ability of teachers is to have them attend a parent-centered activity at the school that is disorganized or poorly planned. This will cause parents to think that if the activities they are attending are poorly planned and operated, then the level of instruction within classrooms can't be much better.

Any time parents come to a conference, event, or activity, it should be thoroughly organized. When parents visit classrooms they should not leave feeling like the event or activity was a waste of their time. When parents feel this way, it is detrimental for the school because not only do those parents leave dissatisfied, they will share those same feelings with other parents, which will distort their views and feelings about the school.

Whenever teachers invite parents to the school for any reason, they must make sure the experience is not only a pleasant one, but also one that is efficient and organized. Teachers can't control the experience that parents have every time they come to the school, but they can control the experience when parents are summoned to the school on their behalf. Most of the time when parents visit the school, it is due to contact made by classroom teachers—whether it is for a conference, brief meeting, school event, or classroom visit. If the teachers in a given school building collectively work to ensure that their respective interactions with parents are well planned and organized, the level of parental engagement will improve tremendously throughout the entire school building.

Parent Recognition

One aspect of parental engagement that is often overlooked by teachers and administrators alike is recognizing parents for their contributions to their child's educational development. This is overlooked because most education professionals don't see the point in rewarding parents for something they should naturally do for their children. This type of thinking isn't beneficial for establishing strong ties with parents.

Everyone likes to feel appreciated and rewarded for their efforts, and parents are no different. The recognition that teachers could give to parents will strengthen the parents' ties with the school and the classroom teacher. Giving parents recognition will also help close the distance that often exists between the classroom and the students' homes. Parents will feel more invested and connected to the school. The following are some positive ways teachers can acknowledge parents:

- Give out parent awards and certificates.
- Send thank you letters, e-mails, or postcards to parents.
- Verbally acknowledge parents during assemblies and other meetings.
- Encourage parents to join committees and take on leadership roles within the school.
- Offer incentives for the first fifty parents who show up for a school-sponsored event.

This list is not exhaustive. The main idea behind acknowledging parents is to make them feel good about the school, their child's teacher, and the role they play in their child's educational development. Parental engagement is something that public schoolteachers must pursue constantly. Happy and engaged parents make for more productive students and productive teachers. Parents can become a teacher's best ally.

SUMMARY POINTS

- Teachers must diligently work to gain parents' trust and establish rapport.
- Teachers should be the ones to initiate contact with parents.
- Parent contact should be made early and often.
- When calling parents, try to have at least one positive thing to say about the student.
- Teachers should communicate with parents in many forms (e.g., letters, phone calls, conferences, e-mails, text messages, etc.).
- Make sure that every event, conference, and activity where parents are invited is well planned and organized.
- Teachers should give parents awards and recognition for the work they contribute to the classroom environment whenever possible.

CONCLUSION
Elements of Effective Teaching

A commonly accepted notion within the educational community is that teaching is more art than science. While this may be true on many levels, certain elements and principles can be repeated over time that can add up to a winning teaching formula.

The following elements of effective teaching (EETs) are commonly overlooked or devalued by many teaching professionals. The reasons these elements are overlooked vary with each individual teacher, but one thing is for certain: The consistent use of these elements combined with the Cleopatra Teacher Rules will give public schoolteachers the ability to reach all students at all learning levels in an effective manner. They will also help teachers improve on their personal practice within the classroom, helping them to not only become master educators, but also to set the tone to become leaders within their respective school communities.

EET I: USING QUESTIONS TO ENHANCE A LESSON

Using questions as part of one's instructional design has been credited to the classical Greek philosopher Socrates (469–399 BC). He would ask his students a series of questions about a topic or concept to get them to arrive at the right answer, and to get students to think deeply about the issues associated with a topic. Socrates understood long ago that using questions during a lesson helps enhance students' understanding of the content. Asking questions also fosters critical thinking, which allows students to think about the content abstractly, which is a higher order skill.

This EET directly ties in with the second and third Cleopatra Teacher Rules. During a given lesson, teachers should ask a minimum of ten different questions. Teachers should also call on a variety of students in the classroom, not just the ones who regularly volunteer. This will allow students to think about the concepts being taught in different ways; it will increase their understanding, allowing them to arrive at conclusions without having the teacher give them the answers, and help to improve the overall learning atmosphere within the classroom.

Also, when asking questions, teachers should deliberately call on students who don't raise their hands. Doing so will help keep the entire class engaged and participating during the lesson.

EET2: CHECKING FOR STUDENTS' MISUNDERSTANDINGS

Checking for students' misunderstandings is important because some students aren't able to fully master a skill or develop a deeper understanding of a topic simply because they didn't completely understand it: They may have mastered some parts of the lesson but not all. This happens because most teachers only gather feedback from students in two ways: First, they rely on the questions that students ask them. If the students' questions indicate a lack of understanding, then they will address the issue. Second, most teachers gather feedback from students after a unit test or summative assessment. These two methods for gathering feedback on students are fine, but if they are a teacher's primary method, the teacher may not be consistently effective.

Teachers who only rely on the two aforementioned methods of gathering feedback from students will consistently miss the students who don't volunteer to ask questions, and those who behave demurely. Also, waiting to view summative assessment data will not be helpful if the teacher doesn't go back and reteach the concepts where students are deficient. When summative assessments are given, teachers are usually trying to arrive at a grade for their students, so it's very likely that they will move on to the next unit or concept, while the students remain deficient in a particular area.

Teachers can alleviate this problem by checking for students' misunderstanding consistently throughout a lesson. This effective teaching element connects with the second and third Cleopatra Teacher Rules. While students are engaged in an interesting lesson that is connected to their learning styles, teachers can walk around the room to monitor students' work. Teachers can also have students demonstrate what they know by having them work problems on the board, or verbally explain what they have learned in their own words. Teachers can also give students short-cycle assessments at different stages during a unit. This will give teachers the ability to assess what students know before arriving at a final grade.

EET3: DIFFERENTIATED INSTRUCTION

All effective teachers differentiate their classroom instruction. This is done every time teachers modify their lessons and activities to meet the various needs of students in the classroom. Teachers will encounter students with various learning levels and cognitive abilities. Therefore, they will not be able to deliver the same lessons, in the same manner, to all students at the same time. This doesn't mean that teachers have to prepare several different lesson plans for individual students in the class. The same lesson, or unit, can be taught to all students, but the teacher may have to adjust it according to the individual deficiencies of some of the students.

This could mean that more advanced students are given higher-order tasking and activities to keep them moving forward, while lower functioning students are given appropriate tasks that meet their needs and keep them progressing as well. This EET goes back to the first and third Cleopatra Teacher Rules: Know Your Students and Teach Interesting Lessons. These rules talk about how important planning is to a teacher's lesson. To differentiate instruction effectively, teachers must know students' needs, deficiencies, and strengths; then they will be able to accurately adjust their lessons and plan accordingly so that all students are moving forward.

EET4: CO-GENERATIVE INSTRUCTION

Once teachers have developed a strong understanding of the first four Cleopatra Teacher Rules, they can progress toward what I have coined as *co-generative instruction* (CI). This is not be confused with *co-teaching*. Co-teaching is when two or more instructors collaborate on the design and implementation of lessons and activities within a classroom setting. Co-generative instruction is entirely different. It involves having the classroom teacher collaborate with students to design, implement, and deliver instruction. This approach gives students greater opportunities to connect with the content in a genuine way, and allows them to take ownership of their learning.

This is a very powerful way to combine all of the aforementioned strategies mentioned in this book (i.e., building trust and rapport, making genuine connections, being a facilitator, teaching interesting lessons, and establishing a student-centered atmosphere in the classroom that is conducive to learning). Co-generative instruction allows students to become active participants within the learning process, fostering the deepest level of investment from them. It also gives students a voice in the teaching and learning process, allowing them to express themselves in uncharacteristic ways, and communicate their understanding of the content in their own language and terminology. This strengthens their understanding of the concepts and skills because it fosters a genuine dialogue between students and teachers.

Co-generative instruction is not something that teachers should use every day, nor is it something that novice or inexperienced teachers should try without a thorough understanding of the students' cognitive levels and behaviors. For co-generative instruction to work effectively, teachers must not only have a keen understanding of their students, but they must completely communicate and confirm the expectations and parameters of the assignment with students.

EET5: WORKING WITH COLLEAGUES

It is well within the parameters of a teacher's job to collaborate with colleagues, work as a team player, learn from those who may have more experience, and connect with people who have been in the school longer. It is also good to share ideas, best practices, and co-teach when appropriate. Such actions make reporting to work more pleasant, and it contributes to the overall culture of the entire school community. As stated previously, teachers can't do it alone; they are going to need allies to assist them at various points in their careers. A supportive teacher colleague is one of the best allies a teacher can have in their corner. But all public schoolteachers need to understand this: Under no circumstances should they allow themselves to be corrupted or co-opted by their colleagues for the sake of working cooperatively, nor should they ever participate in a divisive group.

It's unfortunate, but the reality in many public school districts—especially those with a history of failure—is that they are littered with individuals who have low morale, negative attitudes, and divisive spirits. These individuals are detrimental to anyone trying to really make a difference, and do what's best for students and the overall school community. What makes matters worse is that some of these individuals have the power to influence the actions and opinions of others within the school building. This is especially dangerous for novice teachers and those who are new to a particular school. They end up being influenced in the wrong manner, taking on the negative characteristics of such individuals out of fear of being ostracized. This is especially true for young teachers because most of them are too naïve to know or understand how they are being manipulated and corrupted.

This is why teachers must have a solid grasp of their own educational philosophy and core beliefs. This is the only way they will be able to withstand such negative influences and still do what is right in the name of effective teaching and learning. Understand: It is okay to work with colleagues, but it is not okay to be worked over by colleagues. Stay away from people with divisive spirits and negative attitudes. They will only pull you down and dampen your resolve for the work you have to do as an education professional.

EET6: CONTINUE TEACHING UNTIL THE END OF THE SCHOOL YEAR

It is not uncommon to find that most public schools take a huge sigh of relief after their state's standardized tests have been administered. So much emphasis was put on testing for the entire year that now that it is over and the school year is coming to a close, everyone in the entire school community is literally ready to celebrate. Most schools celebrate by going on field trips, hosting activity days, and having food parties, just to name a few events.

Those things are all fine, but they could have some detrimental effects on students if teachers are not mindful. Because so many fun activities are taking place toward the end of the school year, many teachers stop teaching and delivering quality instruction as well. Instead of continuing to teach interesting lessons, they have classroom parties; show noninstructional movies and cartoons; bring in junk food several times per week; take students outside for extra recess; or give students more "free time" to talk, play games, or use the computer in a noninstructional way.

When teachers behave in this manner, they are not only negatively affecting the work they've done with students all year, but are also affecting what teachers will have to deal with from students the next year. Many students don't receive quality instruction of any kind during the summer months of June, July, and August, so when teachers take off in late April or early May, this potentially adds two extra months of noninstruction. It's no wonder many students returning to school after summer break don't retain the concepts taught to them the previous year.

This is why public schoolteachers must continue to teach all the way to the end of the school year. Students truly need the instruction to help cement the concepts they learn so that it stays with them. Instead of taking off early, teachers can either reteach some of the concepts that students struggled with prior to the standardized test, or they can start students on concepts they'll see next school year in the next grade.

EET7: ALWAYS SEEK TO IMPROVE YOUR TEACHING PROWESS

The best teachers are able to create a conducive classroom environment, and model developmentally appropriate learning, when they are in a continuous learning process themselves. Too many teachers will not do anything to advance their own learning and teaching practice unless it is required of them. They will not take any college courses, read a book, or attend any education-related seminars unless they are receiving some kind of credit toward recertifying their teaching credentials. The only professional development and training they receive are the few sessions required by their respective school districts.

Public schoolteachers need to take more control over their own learning, growth, and development. They should attend seminars, conferences, and training sessions offered outside of their school districts. They should also read books, magazines, and other educational publications connected to their work and to the issues faced by teachers locally and around the country. Doing so will inform their decision making, improve their practice, and keep them on the cutting edge of best practices occurring in the field of education. This will also help teachers generate new and fresh ideas connected to their lessons and the teaching and learning process.

REFERENCES

Flamarion, E. (1993). *Cleopatra: The life and death of a pharaoh.* New York: Harry Abrams Publishers.

Graziano, C. (2005). Public education faces a crisis in teacher retention, *Edutopia.* Retrieved December 2012 from http://www.edutopia.org/schools-out.

Jackson, R. R. (2011). *How to plan rigorous instruction.* Alexandria, VA: ASCD.

Johnson, L. (2011). *Teaching outside the box: How to grab your students by their brains,* ed 2. Hoboken, NJ: Jossey-Bass.

Kain, E. (2011). High teacher turnover rates are a big problem in America, *Forbes.* Retrieved December 2012 from http://www.forbes.com/sites/erikkain/2011/03/08/high-teacher-turnover-rates-are-a-big-problem-for-americas-public-schools/

Kaiser, B., & Rasminsky, S. (2007). *Challenging behavior in young children.* Upper Saddle River, NJ: Pearson.

Kohn, A. (1999). *The schools our children deserve.* Boston: Houghton Mifflin.

Levy, H. M. (2008). Meeting the needs of all students through differentiated instruction: Helping every child reach and exceed standards. *The Clearing House, 81* (4), 161–164.

Lieberman, D. (2000). *Get anyone to do anything: Never feel powerless again.* New York: St. Martin's/Griffin.

Mangrum, J. (2010). Sharing practice through Socratic seminars. *Kappan, 91* (7), 40–43.

McDonald, E., & Hershman, D. (2010). *Classrooms that spark: Recharge and revive your teaching,* ed 2. Hoboken, NJ: Jossey-Bass.

Miller, R., & Browning, S. (2008). *Ancient world leaders: Cleopatra.* New York: Chelsea House.

Nardo, D. (2001). *Cleopatra.* Farmington Hills, MI: Greenhaven.

Partin, R. (2009). *The classroom teacher's survival guide,* ed 3. Hoboken, NJ: Jossey-Bass.

Pateman, R. (1994). *Cultures of the world: Egypt.* Tarrytown, NY: Marshall Cavendish.

Pritchard, A. (2008). *Ways of learning: Learning theories and learning styles in the classroom.* New York: David Fulton Books.

Pilonieta, P., & Medina, A. (2009). Reciprocal teaching for the primary grades: We can do it too! *The Reading Teacher, 63* (2), 120–129.

Ritchhart, R., & Church, M. (2011). *Making thinking visible: How to promote engagement, understanding, and independence for all learners.* Hoboken, NJ: Jossey-Bass.

Roller, D. (2010). *Cleopatra.* Oxford, UK: Oxford University Press.

Sapet, K. (2007). *Cleopatra: Ruler of Egypt.* Greensboro, NC: Morgan Reynolds.

Taylor, L., & Parsons, J. (2011). Improving student engagement. *Current Issues in Education, 14* (1), 5.

Tyldesley, J. (2008). *Cleopatra: The last queen of Egypt.* New York: Basic Books.

Weiner, L. (2003). Why is classroom management so vexing to urban teachers? *Theory into Practice, 42* (4).

White, M., Crouse, A., Bafile, C., & Barnes, H. (2009). *Extraordinary teachers: Teaching for success.* Englewood, CO: Lead Learn Press.

Yisrael, S. *Classroom management: A guide for urban school teachers.* Lanham, MD: Rowman & Littlefield Education, 2012.

SOURCES CONSULTED

Beard, C., & Wilson, J. (2006). *Experiential learning: A best practice handbook for educators and trainers.* Philadelphia: Kogan Page.

Brown, D. (2003). Urban teachers' use of culturally responsive management strategies. *Theory into Practice, 42* (4), 277.

Cambourne, B. (1989). *Theory into practice: The whole story.* Gosford, Australia: Ashton Scholastic.

Fosnot, C. (2005). *Constructivism: Theory, perspectives, and practice.* New York: Teachers' College Press.

Harder, R., Orlich, D., Callahan, R., Trevisan, M., Brown, A., & Miller, D. (2012). *Teaching strategies: A guide to effective instruction,* ed 10. New York: Wadsworth Cengage Learning.

Highet, G. (1989). *The art of teaching.* New York: Vintage Books.

Hoobler, D., & Hoobler, T. (1988). *Cleopatra.* New York: Chelsea House.

Kemmis, S., Cole, P., & Suggett, D. (1983). *Orientations to curriculum and transition: Towards the socially-critical school.* Melbourne: Victorian Institute of Secondary Education.

Kunjufu, J. (2002). *Black students and middle class teachers.* Sauk Village, IL: African American Images.

Lundgren, U. (1983). *Between hope and happening: Text and context in curriculum.* Geelong, Australia: Deakin University Press.

The National Center for Education Statistics. Retrieved from www.nces.ed.gov

ABOUT THE AUTHOR

Dr. Sean B. Yisrael began his career in public education in 1997 as a social studies teacher. In 2004, he left the classroom to enter the ranks of school administration. Dr. Yisrael has worked as a school administrator in various school districts located in Ohio and the District of Columbia. In 2010, Dr. Yisrael formed Education Practitioners for Better Schools (EPBS), a professional development company designed to provide professional enrichment services to school district employees and childcare providers.

Also in 2010, Dr. Yisrael signed with Rowman and Littlefield. Since then he has published a total of five educational books. Other titles include *Classroom Management: A Guide for Urban School Teachers, The Hard Truth: Problems and Issues Affecting Urban School Reform, The 12 Laws of Urban School Leadership*, and *The Warrior Principal: New Leadership for Urban Schools.* He has traveled the country giving speeches and book talks to parents, teachers, and school administrators.

Dr. Yisrael is a lecturer, scholar, and author, but most importantly, he is an educator who is passionate about working to ensure that all students attending public schools receive a quality education regardless of their family's background or socioeconomic status. Dr. Yisrael can be reached at www.seanyisrael.com or via email at sean@seanyisrael.com.